"Speak properly and in few words as you can, but always plainly, for the end of speech is not ostentation, but to be understood"

—from More Fruits of Solitude by William Penn.

RISING TO MEET OUR TRANSFORMATION

WILLIAM E LEAHY

Order this book online at www.trafford.com
or email orders@trafford.com

Most Trafford titles are also available at major online book retailers.

Printed in the United States of America.

ISBN: 978-1-4907-2091-3 (sc)
ISBN: 978-1-4907-2105-7 (hc)
ISBN: 978-1-4907-2092-0 (e)

Library of Congress Control Number: 2013922361

Trafford rev. 01/23/2014

 www.trafford.com

North America & international
toll-free: 1 888 232 4444 (USA & Canada)
fax: 812 355 4082

Rising to Meet Our Transformation
Preface

Eventually we all arrive at our own physical, mental or spiritual transformation. At the point in time when we arrive change abounds everywhere and we conform to it or perish.It is our connectivity to others that often propels us to change since we are so closely knit and desire to be in oneness.

Although there are several types of transformations we may not accomodate all these various changes in our lives. We can rebel and fight cultural change while it is happening to declare our chosen independence for a while. Yet some transformations invented by each worldly culture will force us to change and rearrange our lives. All state members will conform to a desired image or the culture police will make it happen despite our protests.

Transformation aligns to constant culture readaption and reforming. Great rolling waves will come crashing onto our beaches. Often we must grab flotation devices to remain upside and adroitly manuever so we do not get caught in the undertow. Hence we will eventually rise to meet our transformation literally and figuratively.

In my mind I see us all changing in the many different facets of our lives going forward. Thus I wrote my words as a testimony to various changes evolving or developing here. Sometimes it is in a picture I see or often a picture strikes a chord of revision in my mind. My hope is that some poems click in the mind of the reader as events in their own life confirm what has been written.

Enjoy your Transformation!

William Leahy

January 2014

Rising To Meet Our Transformation

Table of contents

Reforging our Many Images

Charge ahead and observe the remarkable creative You

Sculpture a pathway before proceeding to forge ahead

Move cautiously and creatively to your new mindset

Now see how clear a picture becomes without briars

Reforge multitudes of thoughts into a growing image

Team Challenge

Hold onto the walls
Stake a hook to guide
Know the natural feel
Grope carefully ahead
A journey is unfolding
Test a trailing crevice
Discovery is profound
Our ropes hold firm
Compatriots support

MAGNIFICENT CRYSTAL VENTURE

Chime to the Music of the Daily Buzz

Lives are lived in the bodies we are loaned
Taking care of business really belongs to us
No one can enter your flesh form given
Listen to the sounds of your body move about
Ancient music bellows about our days and weeks
Our flesh forms give us the mobility to create
Carefully craft a symphony of ancient chimes
Each note represents a pattern of daily progress
When our loaned bodies give out: leave notepads

Time unfolds a multitude of thoughts about life
How we react to the overpowering crisis before us
Carefully we weave a pattern of protection about
Our objective is to guide all to a safety netting
Sometimes our friends fail to follow the pattern
Panic actions lead some to perilous pathways
Your calm voice calls in the face of red alarm
Masses of independent thinkers disappear below
Self Creative man wallows in his superiority
Oneness of thought can destroy a moving army
Forging down the trail we are missing people
Casualties abound in the dull roar of re-direction.
Follow clear direction or drown in crystal sand

Uncovering My Reality

Up from the uncharted land forms
Behold this rough terrain of land
Sometimes I hike without trails
Therefore I must chart...leave dabs
Building stone layers and Cairns
This for my tracing backward later
My trail map traces human touch
Sharp turns and deep crevices now
They carefully abound on all sides
Walking is treacherous and soft
Test every step before alighting

Pioneering the ledges and steeps
Time may make blood donations
I may slip fall or be compromised
Yet my zeal for adventure drives
Now I come to a blind face wall
My trail must take a new path now
I then unwind the uncharted scape
Destiny requires modification way
New platform rocks show promise
Ahead I see a Native Indian track
See promise will take me forward

Stepping briskly confidence seeps
Since the old walk way exists here
I chart and see it leads onward
Yet in places there are wash outs
Regardless I horizon a guess now
Then I see new beginnings ahead
Finally the river bottom is present
I will call this a Great Zigzag Trail

Tranquility

Presenting a quiet time is meaningful
A great gathering of thoughts for now
We assemble our life story in words
Then we provide a casting dialogue
We have someone play out our role
Only then we see our imperfections
Yet in reality we hide our weakness
We bellow about our great strengths
Tomorrow arrives and we cover all
See I manipulate myself for others
Reality then colors tranquility boldly

Remembering the Lilacs

I will always remember May boughs
How the sudden array of Purple came
The mass of blossom burst spread out
Lilac bushes massed aromas all over
Their smell perfumed the Spring air
Our award for a few days of perfume
Arrange lilacs in white milk glass
vase

The benediction of spring envelops
Enjoy the moments breath of spice
Find a true passion for the mixture
Color this season as rising new birth
Fill the countryside with freshness
I am seeing the lands new foliage
Create a clear image of rebirthing

I view the whole landscape beaming
New shades of pinkpurplerose arise
I witness the world as turning amass
Bright colors change my old attitudes
I focus on the positive purple images
In time the boughs will again fade
Yet for now I can reign in their glory

Grow Yet Grow More

In the prime of my life I now move
A trellis of creation makes me aware
I must grasp new ideas to array them
I must plan and grow brilliance anew
Flow the ideas of resilience forward
I am moving mesas and buttes now
I will move stones to create structures
I am about building a new day edifice
I have foundations built to start solid
Foundations will support my ideas
Ideas will grow on the Promise trees
Trees will spread thought branches
Thought branches have the real /ideas
Promise ideas spring forth as growth
Choose the ideas of lasting change
Harvest ideas from the promise trees
Then grow yet grow more abundantly

Charmed

There are a few people who can schmooz
They develop all these smooth moves
Their actions flow like a special trance
Their whiz words are slow moving glow
Somehow we are captured like statues
Our only action is to seem frozen amazed
When their charmed performance is done
We jabber as crows to listening audiences

Finding My Best Thoughts Beaming

It is my desire to publicize plus positive
Negativity embraces us in a huge crush
Out antenna can only absorb so much
Outrage and denial is the rampant view
Sit in your chair as I count the explosions
Many people pop their upper brain cells
Massive blood pressure rises in multitude
Red faces color the lit screens as scream
The battle cry presents an insanity amass
Continually fire is set and then doused
We are victims of the billowed brainwash
So they yell until they get their own way
Politicians run to cover their wounds now
Ease the pain of sufferers until elections
Senator Snide will side with the loudest
This will carry him to a saintly victory

Yet the final curtain will arise positive
I see an army of truth seekers will arise
My part is to push insanity out into space
The parking lot is space for barking a lot
The press should find barking lots scream
Once we are onto the standing sanity tree
We will find the courage to send leaves
We must send leaves of absence to pitted
Pitted politicians are carrying shields
My hope is real shields will protect sanity
Otherwise slippery slopes leave no hope
My best thoughts beaming should thrive
Messages of truth must prevail in today
Or our culture is doomed to destruction
Beaming messages must counter fallacy
Shields not windshield can wipe out truth
Rise to the moment of truth or perish!

Finding Our Best Routes

I am searching the countryside plainly
Currently I now observe the straight truth
My critical path needs to be best for all
Therefore I will map my lifetime route
Appealing to all I will get true consensus
Perhaps I may not agree with a direction
Yet I should follow the best route known
Many are dependent upon my decisions
As I move my true vision becomes clear
Seek out post pathways to provide for all
We are not alone in our specific universe
Others share our universal space so given
Multitudes rely on all our post pathways
We are the model to others giving breadth
I focus my vision and map the true way
I now know how critical my direction is
Finding and following the route is vital
We are but little lights enlightening all
I see a major roll in cutting a correct path
Rejoice for a map master I share a road
My travel is traced to a final destination

Challenge of the Ages

I roll forward and see my imperfections bleed out of my body since I am out of control and out of strategies
Finding my plan has been a challenge and a great enterprise since I see life differently than the mainstream
Bellowing from my place of comfort I must find discomfort in my self only then will I begin major revision
Charging forward the clock is running at an alarming pace so I need to be aware and ready to reshape and redo
Running now I have sought wisdom which will allow me to reformat my life into a masterful new complexity
Pour forth the new thought waves of authenticity and originality as I follow the new path appearing before me
Now I see that adjustments and reprocessing needed to erect a positive plan of lasting persistence as I gallop
Yes I gallop and stretch and stride forward with the going gait and get ready to embrace a massive revision
Finding the correct pace I have begun my campaign to erase the lingering past and take note of the finite future
Specific plans need to be stashed in the allowance bag of expectation and ingenuity to be worked swiftly now
Find pieces and parts of the dynamics that work in unison and compel these critical masses to weld in oneness
I am about creating a new being I am about creating a new approach I am about revising repacking the new me

Into the Gardens of Life I see the Bounty

See the marvels of the fields of bounty as the harvest repeats its wonder and propels the seeds of life to create sustenance
How the seeds do thrive in the loam soils of nature that subside in the edges and rows that are mulched and fed constantly
Relish the work of dedicated farmers who work the lush fields to provide the yields of plenty for the masses of humanity
Our life's bounty is given from the organic rows that generate the green plasma that feeds the massive planets populations
We are fully blessed by these anointed farmers who love and respect the landscape that is carefully and quietly manicured
Rise up rejoice with the bountiful harvest, our hearts and souls are nourished from the Garden of Eden's great abundance

Search the horizon...for the great harvest of life passes on for miles and miles as we fill the barns overflowing to then wait
Wait and listen as the land will deep sleep into a winter solstice and remain in a frozen bed until a Great robin sings Spring

COME THEN NOW ENJOY THE WATER

See the gushing water
Ahead it peals quickly
After my short dry walk
Water appeals my soul
At last I lick the rocks
The wet gushing water fills my soul like a balloon
I was empty and dry and refreshing water fills me
What have I done to escape the dryness of today?
There were others in need so I assisted them
The road ahead split and I gave them directions

The road was filled with debris so then I removed it
The road was filled with marauders and I shielded it
The road had deep potholes so I tarred and filled them
The road was narrow in places I expanded its width
The road ended in places so I found many detours
The road had sharp briars on the side so I cut them
The road was marked with pain so I healed them
The road was called El Camino Real and I noted it
When the time came to leave I reminded them of this
When the power of compassion enables you to act
Take action and come then now and enjoy the water

Cast your Bread

Once I saw a Deliverance Angel
Clarity held me in a tranced state
Each time I sought to gain wisdom
The Icon message repeated itself
"Cast your bread upon the waters
After many days you will find it"
Why did I observe this allegory?
Why did I observe this message?
When all below fails seek it above

Wisdom filters into our lives once
Messages are written on our walls
They are seen on new street signs
Words are on a side of buildings
Observe an etching on monuments
Buildings do not speak and walls
fail to continually communicate
Icons do not speak streets blank us
Yet subtle messages arrive clearly
Translate wisdom in your serenity

FINDING THE DRY FLATLAND

Just ahead I see flat desert plains
They meander over the landscape
There is quiet serenity surrounding
Nothing moving will escape notice
Even the waving Orange Ocotillo

Flat desert plains have no hiding
Even the occasional arroyo sees
The eyes of the desert are keen
Survival in hot deserts is terminal
Finding a ramada shield is new life

Without a protective force: Chaos
Traversing on dry deserts is quick
Water becomes immediate staples
Find your dry heat blasting now
Your compass leading: be accurate

Blistering heat boils your brains
Locate your flatland destination
Find your reason find true treasure
Trace back your trail to El Dorado
Water my hope ahead I see a mirage

Our Parranza

We escape lifes narrows through light
Ahead is the prime passage parranza
Openings lead us around the crevice
We are the survivors of red canyons
Instincts guide us to narrow passages
observing ahead we see faint shadows
We slip through a deliverance ahead
All destinations to welcome light now
A great Parranza has allowed us life
Our grateful trail master led us ahead
Now we must traverse an opening
Challenge ourselves to find a groove
Climb with great resolve to escape
Journey through rock formations now
Locate the waving persistent patterns
Grab onto the sandstone structures
Our continuing existence is in sand
Either we write upon sand or conquer
Our conquest leads us to an opening
The great Passage of life echoes now
A cave window can be very confining
Passages of great light a sign of hope
We live a sea of defined hopefulness
Find passage though Life's Parranza

Find The Pictures of Life's Learning

Little lessons in life arise and return to reinforce our lack of focus and compassion
I intend to change and revise my thinking but I am frozen in my old resolute ways
Now I must pick up the new spontaneous idea of change then reorder my thinking
Otherwise I will remain static and become part of an extinct sabertooth civilization

Sabino Canyon Alive

My first view of Sabino Canyon was seeing water gush out into a desert
Water was to refresh the dim, dried and dismal plants parched by heat
Powerful waves of sun beamed rays radiate in Sonoran desert flatlands
I am greatly arid and paled without the Sabino Canyon rushing waters
Blasting from the mountaintop the rain and snow melt feeds the dryland
Recalling the streams of relief I stand and greet the massive desert flow
How quickly Life can fade in the Sonoran inferno without life substance
Pour forth in excitement and vigor to refresh the massive dry landscape
Water is the source of continuing existence treasure its natural vital links
We are just sojourners passing through the exulted Ocotillo and Saguaro

The Gardens

Masses of color have commenced and painted an image of quietude
Along the edge of the water I observe a reflection of the autumns peace
Once one maple tree sends the word about a massive color collage- Zam
A burst of many shades fill the countryside quickly and repeat over
Gloss into the many images of the countryside; many autumns are gone
Now you and I may be entering the remaining autumns of our existence
Observe how groomed and prepared that the garden of life has become
Autumn is a time of lasting fulfillment a real signature of our lifes work
Are your papers ready? your words honed into the people surrounding?
Now is the time of completion, now is a time of preparation...Act now!

Parallel

We parallel the bar of life and find our purpose in the many intregal acts
We are called upon to do great leaps forward...accommodate the masses
At other times we are encouraged to do flips when everyone else flops
Then we perform somersaults when family members get into trouble
Often times without knowing we traverse the slide first to get it clean
Of course we do a cartwheel for the visiting relatives to allow for peace
We cannot forget to carefully pull strings when our children are unhappy
We perfect a push to glide swing sets for our precious grandchildren
Once we have made all these parallels we get a four star rank going up

See Miracles Happen

Sometimes we see small miracles
Often we ignore the vivid message
How outrageous a pool of tadpoles
What are they doing on my pathway
Their miracle a new frog generation
A few miles further desert bighorns
In the herd are new yearlings aware
They are the desert sheep of choice
Then further I discover a busy beaver
She has built a massive mudpack den
Her young will come soon to bear
Soon I see a herd of new mule deer
They cautiously move to drink water
One will be alert to dangerous sounds
Then a final miracle occurs ahead
Torrents of rain come to fill the land
Nature needs to replenish the plants
Vegetation needs to drink for life
In the arid desert water is a miracle
Monsoon downpours occur irregular
Raging torrents is natures desert dew
Water miracles baptize the country.

Remove Your Clock

Time has great value to us mortals
Often I see that it races too quickly
Yet I am courageous in my thinking
I can accomplish all I set for today
My goals fall short and run beyond
Today remained as a gazelle racing
Therefore I need to lower my goals
Hence I need to shorten expectations
My radical idea is to remove clocks
Time may pass at a slower pace then
This solution:so empty time wins out
Whatever talent I have now acquired
I must allow for all creativity to flow
My creative powers are time limited
I cannot move quicker than my ideas
Allow creativity its window of time
I maintain sanity at creations wheel

Fly By The Seat of My Pants

I noticed my pants have no seat attached
Thus I must fly by continuous belt loops
Belt loops have string affixed to balloons
Then I will arise above all with helium
Gas is the means to allow the wind to lift
Then I will see what is missing below
Small figures will move to lifes chime
The human map peopled below amazing
Once we see the irregular patterns of life
Life takes on new meaning with a view
Maybe change is possible in the future
I need to fly by the belt loops more often

Replanting Life

There will come a time of closeness
Discovering the raw crush of people
I become replanted in the wilderness
Moving was my option to consider
I see the need to reconnect for others
Multitudes surround my living space
I remain sparse to allow for growth
No formula can sketch my success
Yet there was an urge to now reform
Half my life will be soon spent here
Whatever my decision for regrowth
Only that the original planting did not
I will now arise and send new sprouts
My replanting was a desert miracle
My now plan to ensure all will grow
I will grow to reach upper extremes
Today the slow accession will change
I will grow in quick ascension now
Tomorrow will be a Replanting time
Now enter the joy of positive renewal

Ovation

Let us now rise and see how we glow
Major images flash across our path
As we stand we are observing light
We have been enlightened by crowds
Masses of people will encourage us
Perhaps they are clapping for real joy
If we recognize they are enthusiastic
If we see revision we will embrace it
If we become serious change happens
I need to see the extraordinary spark
I need to be exceptionally positive
I need to allow time for change now
I receive an ovation for my attitude
I receive the award for performance
I receive massive clap encouragement
I will perform the best action known
I will get the intricacies all ironed out
I will get my total challenges mapped
I can improve the swing song of life
I can remake all my former steps now
I can visualize my next best transfer
I may succeed in accomplishing redo
I may allow for energy to overwhelm
I may proclaim victory as I arise now
My ovation is now richly deserved
My ovation has deep map meaning
My ovation was for true completion
Perform life as it was your total task
Perform your act as a stellar motion
Perform life as with the curtain call

The Race of Life is Moving

Quickly I am running a race in time
A baton is passed to me... I respond
Following the streets and roads ahead
Often there are detours and I do miss
Sometimes new trails beckon I miss
New ventures happen no matter what
Prepare for change-rearrange-reform
A Lifetime of revision is beginning
Sometimes I am paralyzed to redo it
I must rethink my role and rise to it
Multitudinal tasks and nodes are here
Climb upward to fill the interstices
Let no spaces prevail as to unknown
It is my regard to become a meteor
Charge across to sky of persuasion
Convince those wavering to move
Now I am riding the new road waves
I will ride and run the given pathway
The race has moved and life goes on

Rhapsody En masse

A song that is familiar rings in my ear
My hollow head echoes the melody
Slowly a rising crescendo reverberates
Familiar notes play a symphony here
Others arise and listen from a distance
Soon the whole countryside hears music
A steady beat rises and grows ahead
Constant rising repetitious ringing plays
Knowingly I am inspired to allow peace
At once serenity overlaps my total being
The swing song is driven to higher notes
A bellowing chorus of music bursts out
Massive chimes of Bolero shock waves
Waves become the banner of believing
A massive rhapsody of rising river wash
My ears have been artfully sculpted now
A revelation of Ravel has risen in power
I hear the blare of Bolero beckoning now
A grand finale leads me to raw revision
A great rolling rhapsody has taken over
At a finality my brain plugged En masse

Following the Inspiration

Creation begins with inspiration leading
It is not unknown if inventors are assured
They reason their ideas on several notes
Once they know their experiment moves
Charging ahead they plug the main pittle
The pittle fails to respond so troubleshoot
Troubleshoot shows raw umbrage power
Raw Amber is reconnected to plentystone
Plentystone does not generate... only poo
One second look shows burned wire ends
Wire to nowhere fails to work Re-Inspire

KEEPING THE CAP

Seek the top of the mountain; Hike to seek the world views
Wrap yourself in excitement; Gaze upon all you see ahead
Conquer the moment in time; Allow forward thinking now
Picture where you want to be; Find the answer and settle it

PROFOUND DIRECTION IS EMERGING FOR YOU

Never be scrambled, every event has a profound meaning
Follow the true North of your compass direction emerging
Allow for some deviation since a true reading is arising
Listen to the powerful needle flowing and begin a journey!!

THE TIGER HAS A THREATENING GROWL AT NOON

Remember the sound you heard and trembled in perilous fright
Was this the roar you had always expected or was it just noise
Remember that unique sound you heard may have been hunger
Yet if we think inwardly our mind should recall all wild growls
Wild growls occur to comfort the shortages that may surround us
Have we begun to recognize the random sound and cries abound
Senses tell us danger is brewing when we hear a troubled alarm
We are given a mind to assist to resolve all threats coming now
Plug all your major chords into play as dangers alarm is evident
Climb the trellis to see what is lurking in the emerging shadows
Our whole identity and imprint is at risk until we can neutralize
Mission one is to stabilize our surroundings and create the calm
Armies of Tigers can create the message of confusion and fear
People of the Wisdom can flex and translate containment Now

Believe in Progress Arising

Progress rings a bell of hope to all
Primary populations arise to a call
Powerful messages pass by a wall
Handwritten scrolls will fail to fall
Charging armies are ready to maul
Direction from power drops a ball
Unintended message rakes a stall
People need quests freedoms hall

March to the banners of new hope
Rearrange houses allow us to cope
Government needs a remake slope
Recreate new laws beyond a grope

Charge to the drum of new sender
develop a mindset for a defender
Words will flow to finally render
Magnificent verbs waves blender
Start real structures to engender
We don't want a new pretender

Press on to Wisdom Tree

Ideas grow on tomorrows brains
Running quicker than bullet trains
Massive power alights to rash lanes
Spinning faster than weather vanes
Climb into new age water mains
Observe a flow of monsoon rains
Power is creating massive strains
Locate safety tracing net drains
Sit on a horse overlook the plains
Ply a moment observe the cranes
Look at your arms see the veins
Power of our muscles give strains
Sometime we create extreme pains
Over time see our power wanes
Rush forward for a moments gains
We all all heading for new Spains
Yelling we come to see our banes
Tomorrow we will chug our canes
Seek wisdom prior to end reigns

Find the Calming Arbor

Constantly we brave the zap wind
Elements of chaos gather to upend
Buttress the circle and then ascend
Fly the banner paramounts defend

Walk a pathway to secure the calm
Discover peace way without harm
Investigate the magnet date palm
See Palm fronds as a symbolic arm

We need to find protected harbors
Locate those with climbing arbors
Learning will create cool salvers
Surround clusters to plaid barbers

Shave your old thought in a clip
Learn quickly and avoid the whip
Finding new ideas wrapped in zip
Aim toward creating a new toe grip

Hang on we are drifting wizards
Moving quicker than sleek lizards

Results are evolving

See how we accomplish little
We fritter away blocks of time
Challenge comes to completion
Our internal clock runs quickly
Prepare your accomplishment
Prepare the precious ten minutes
Time has a way for tiny makeups
Bound forward with fast focus
your phalanges will beat the clock
Time can yet be sometimes sought
However time cannot be bought

Perpetrated

Some people will try to frame you
Others will work hard to tame you
Mainstream folks live in the now
Plain folks understand the how
Remember that noisy cattle call
People were looking at the wall
Discover your talent from afar
Riding to success in a fast car

Be made aware that blame has legs
Your enemies perpetrate the dregs
Finding you the candidate of Fate
Anger will find its remap to hate
Consider how the new story unravels
Their mission fines you at the gavels
Judge will mainly grump and deplore
You have 5 minutes: seek to implore
Now there is very little to explore
There remains little to arise and adore

Climb to the upper veranda and state
Your enemies arose through the gate
You moved ahead and passed in late
They dove through to set a new date
Charge to the tune of Mondays clatter
Run ahead and seek the real matter
Hit hard our heads shake as a platter
Find relief : Stand up to life's batter

Trying my Best

I have shuttled ahead to evenness
I understand the makeup of plans
Marvelous plans encumber time
Wisdom and thought is expected
I may not be included yet I vision

Frost the Windshields and Stairs

Our time unfold in the dark deep cold
Groping we address the frost as a mold
Scraping and sanding removes the rime
Carefully we consider accidents in time
We are the brave and hardy northern pack
Existing now on the mighty power track
Picking up our load before it explodes
Finding safety before in case it implodes
Our lives are living on the narrow gates
One mistake and we are bound by fates
Best practice to best moves melts the ice
Existence worth more than a roll of dice

Driving the Change before us

Running blazing ahead as meteors flying
Whipping across the paths we are volatile
Time's window observes a flash of light
Quickly we dance across liquid horizons
Catapulting ahead stopping not an option
Our civilization is a massive flutter chain
Make noise and the rest of world listens
Our Creation is the babble others hear
Striking a match madness ensues a wave
We set the world on fire with a fiery buzz
Waves of fire send messages to outposts
Outposts scream for a powerful freedom
Action of dawns liberty to many amazed
Communications networks fuels change
Evolutionary change is forming hearts
Change will restructure the planetary top
New possibilities to revolutionary moves
Revolutionary change has evolved now
Now A driving force of change before us
Now the driving change has coalesced
We are living in the New Formation Fold
Get ready for the rising metamorphosis
You are about to become a world number.

Transformation

Constantly I remind Myself of change
Knowing it will come then I rearrange
Challenge is a huge battle and strange
I am too comfortable to mentally derange
Then I will back step and find the range
Tomorrow I reset the clock to prearrange

Unfreeze the Positive thoughts

We rebel sometimes to the notes of good
Why did we not participate in greatness?
Sometimes tunnel vision blocks our view
Our temperament is roiled on few words
Cancel the words and reopen the mindset
Good deeds or good actions assist vision
Open an eye readjust and unfreeze panes

Bursting Forward

My best potential is to be real and patient
Being a creature of instantaneous spur
I unfold as a wild mad hatter running
My helter skelter action locks in a maze
There are too many dead ends to stop at
Escape is not part of my good action plan
I often need spurious guidance to redirect
I need to redirect and re deflect actions
Positive creation will provide a new vista
Send forth a re-plan on my behalf now
There is a bursting of forward ideas now
Awaiting at the redo station I am buzzing

Become the Person

Too often we imitate many others
A real person never once emerges
Trumpets are blaring looking for
Where has the original you gone?
March out of the artificial glow
Arise to a buoyant true personality
Fill the room with joy and jelly
Locate life nourish the audience
Your contingent of best friends are
Friends await one unique message

Larchmont Station

The rapid transit train end stops here
You then take the trolley to Marzipan
You can get a Roastbeef at Zeppys
The Deli closes a one o'clock sharp
The last trolley cruises in at twelve
You should have time to eat and run
Remember to take your acid re ducts
Otherwise perpetual trolley lava roll

Predict a comet path

Racing across a path of night sky
A frosty comet called Ombeaagi
Entering the atmosphere in a flash
It scrapes the late evening solitude
Similar to a match striking flint
Ombeaagi has made its sky spark
What am I searching for above?
Ombeaagi has reached a high flash
In another sixty years it may dance
If it is not burned out it will return
I can dance a tango-stream of dust

Succinctly

This has always been a droopy word
There is no other strong definition as
As specifically we try it stands alone
Then it wanted to be isolated adverb
Brave the solace of distinction alone
You are a word of one single mindset
Character counts very succinctly now
Arise to new mornings new babble

Forge the new view

Come to the flowing river wide
Find the current will run inside
Strong rumbling tension and tide
Should you allow it will then glide
Power of floods will not subside
Await a few days and let it abide
You need to see it run a long stride
After a catastrophe find who died
Rebuilding will restore our pride
Next time a warning do not chide

Charles requiem on a Hill

It became something more then are royal
Over time it became a town that sprung
It sprung and mushroomed out on a river
Many stayed and became new townies
It arose and became named Charlestown
Named after many kings of the same line
A river flowed, revolution occurred here
Breeds Hill embattled beside the Mystic
Residents revere the Mystic ever flowing
Mass monuments arose on Bunker Hill
In Memoriam : Freedom was reborn here

Cleaned Out

I was never quite sure what it meant
Once I heard terms when at card games
Another time Mrs Smyths back yard junk
For me when I was told citrate magnesia
Well then I figured out the true meaning
Cleaning out can be personal and private
But I avoid Magnesia and prefer amnesia
Coming to terms with cleaned out finally
Be quite quiet and do not complain now
Huge benefits assured by being regular.

Protoplasm

The gel of life springs forward now
We are human creatures of living matter
All the life giving cells operate defined
Each cell has a finite purpose and role
As time marches some cells go defunct
Medical mysteries avail and are studied
Time flattens our existence on the earth
Trained medicine men give us some hope
Eventually we become jumbled cell mass
We await the unjumbled jostle machine
Miracles arrive in packets of new plasm
Await now the day of mass rejuvenation
It could arrive twenty minutes too late

Spontaneous Combustion

When we are least aware sparks occur
Waiting for the solitude flames burst
While not paying attention fire bellows
Whereto the charging hot line engulfs

Lobster

Precarious movements in the deep sea moves
Moving like an extraterrestrial being it lunges
Lunges are the bywords of capturing prey
I become prey to my unsuspecting lunges
I need to be careful about planned footwork
Lobsters get caught in the netting trap set
I get caught in lifes web of roaring lions
I must prepare and improve extraterrestially
Otherwise my lobster tail may get broken
I must remain intact before time has been set

Rotunda

Rotunda is synonymous with capitols
We see how ornate they became in time
In time our bodies have molded into
Molded into shapes that are rotund
We mirror image the shapes around us
Prepare for a massive dedication to get
Get a rotund heavyweight a new shape!

Coming Home

Moving away is a new journey discovery
I often think of the distance travelled to
Many times I see images of where I was
Nostalgia does not occur only an image
I remember the over the limit of sauce
Then the words plastered and mocus
We make our own home grown dungeons
Our failure cannot be revived in a bottle
Moving on sometimes allows us space
Victory is in our metamorphous tunnel.

Bleached and Rotting Timbers

Arise on the Arm of Cape Cod
Wasting on sand at Nauset Beach
Extended pieces of bleach timber
Wood planks wear in the harsh sun
Aware of what we now perceive
We ask how many perished here
What raging nor'easter slashed
Crashed ripped apart in sea squalls
Splinters remain of glories passed
The sea swallows men and women
There's no mercy as waves rumble
Boats torn apart in a perilous rage
life is at odds in the savage seas
Whatever we see is dire remains
What survives a valve and pump
Then just jumbled rusted lumber
Final prayer :A cemetery marker
Remembrance in sand AMEN

Illuminay

How the daylight passes quickly and sure
My mind focuses on the illuminay of day
I am self absorbed in rays of good days
Light gives us a trail to seek and follow
At night we stumble and trip over traps
Rise to the new mornings brass bugle
Great messages are alerting the masses
Seek illuminays of days to travel onward
Light life objects move in unison today
Find peace and presence in Illuminay

Profound energy

Seek the low mysterious sound
Passing through I am bound
Often we are directed around
Come close so I here a sound
Patiently howl so we are found
Found abound in a dog pound
We are the lowly Basset Hound
Living famous close to ground

Drive the Morning Forward

Am I marching to the new true melody of the surrounding land
Have I entrusted myself to the pulse of the magical landscape
At once I must blend into the rolling hills and rocky road trails
Then massive mounds and raised beds become part of my soul

Listening to the Mornings Music

Rise to open the near gates that surround our happy compound
Harmonize to the magnificent melodies that fill your quiet soul
Hear the notes of notoriety and allow them to soothe your being
Finding the special tunes that fits your mood for this special day
The mornings music will blend to all the activities of this array
Tomorrow will be more active and may not play as a symphony
Choose the tunes and find the lyrics that flow on a difficult time
Blend the music and prepare the outcomes to match the moods
Now find that the flow of times music will readily ebb and flow
Some music speaks to your heart when the times require peace
Yet another time we may need the hectic sounds that reverberate
Plan the sounds of an open day; each day envelops and blossoms
Listen before the day speaks to your heart then play its music

One Great Educator

I see those who captured my vistas
They grabbed my lurid imagination
Moving they added to my thoughts
Carefully every educator inspires
Quickly they add a flare to re fire
Thus I am set ablaze with new ideas
Astutely they have built a platform
My stage a staircase to rejuvenate
Great brain waves circulate to aide
Assisting closely one educator goes
Going to unleash talent at a bridge
Talent will connect the platforms
Once connected a harvest of words
Great harvests are possible as now
Charging forward I am in position
One great educator introduces it
A massive pouring out connection
I am verbally alive with creativity
Words hit the nails on the out doors
Once hearing.....my message is out

Circulate

Premier Pulsation

One tropical flower sends a message out
Capturing the beauty of the lush island
Rejoice in its isolation and protection
It is hidden for a few to observe in time
Find the passion of lifes memory now
Remember the massive flower blooming
The monstrous flower waved for attention
Did you see a wave of color spray to you?
Open the arches of your soul and paint
Color the memory dots of pink promise
your mind must become attuned to color
The many hues of Paradise will emanate
Initiate your journey with colored boughs
Line the alleyways and hedges brightly
Your marvelous memory is a painted prism
Insure that you take your paint brush along
The final pathway will push into a bouquet
Locate the flowers of Florabunda to begin
Your sojourn is moving a reigning rainbow

Success is Climbing
The Ladder that Matters

We are constantly rising to new hope
There is always more details to observe
What it may be is our continued curiosity
How we react to detailed unknown ways
Climb onto the Querulous Quotient now
Analyze unknown sub atomic particles
Discover the willing wafers of DNA dots
Find the cure for unknown flus and furies
Our hope is the chemistry flask formula
Our journey is in the rejuvenation pills
Someone climbed the ladder to discover
Discover the ladder of genius unleashed
The connective tissue of a few make it
Connectors differ climb and uncover this
Brains evolve and constantly will differ
Fortunately a few will exist and deliver

Mankind will be delivered to sacred vale
Sacred vales will allow for wisdom trees
Once Wisdom trees are planted see glory
everlasting Wisdom trees glorify creation
Creations power permeate peace and joy
Planet Earth needs rejuvenation to grow
Uncover miracles; an evolved mind of Go

Languishing in it

Lives have a real defined purpose
Getting aloft from masses below
One time I stop then am held back
Can I languish where I am to think
Can I languish and then move on
Yes I can and understand problems
Strategize think formulate then act
My life requires languishing first
I must understand the mud puddle
Oh I will arise from roiled waters
Clear thoughts and wisdom assist
Moving I push from the mud slush
Now I begin my defined purpose
My building has begun to progress
See terraces gradings and layouts
Foundations are my clear marking
Advance the main gates to Shalata
I now have key details I proceed
Blueprints of TreVadas now exist
A Colony marked in Open Space
Our initial post planet Cephanoba
Grind the will and wonder ahead
Creative minds do deliver our plan
Erect possibilities in meteor time
Set safety shields and cover pods
Commence to ethereal outer space
Begin to work in light Speed mode
We are the space pioneers in synch
Precision pilots drive spaces quest

Time is Always Upon Us

Reaching I am reminded we have
a profound mission to accomplish
Our journey encompasses a goal
to assist and aid one individual
What are we here for proclaims
the prophetic cry of true service
Sometimes we are unable to assist
just one person in deep quicksand
There will be another appearing
soon on the distant horizon here
Arise and be useful or you will be
forever remaining unaccounted for

Earth Fissures

I see the lines of breaks in the soil crust
This reminds me of how fissures remain
Quietly the earth at times moves inches
When we least expect there are tremors
Tremors occur as the ground swell shakes
I feel the massive reeling and shifting
Nothing under me reigns solid or secure
When I test my brain waves they alter
Now I know the definition of powerless
Absolute undermining of my balance
Where is lands safety netting to hold onto
I am spider prey wafting intact webbing
My escape route is finding web breaks
Hang on to the Trust tree and settle now
My hope is for minor after shock waves
My solace is a subsiding quake forecast

Sunbathing on Clustering Hills

I watched the sun rise slowly, as it
rose it baptized the clustering hills
and set them aglow with majesty

All living objects were sprinkled
with natural fire and were ablaze
then immersed in celestial light

All naked life and limbs were
exposed on the sultry sunbathed
and clustering hills in their youth

I know well the scene on the hills
because I am still breathing and
am willing to tell you about it

Clamoring Calls

Understand the buzz in your ears
You are being called and needed
Clashing, crackling cymbals chime
They are chiming for you right now

Cymbals for an immediate presence
You are needed in many odd places
You remain a hope for the masses
Now you are called to serve multiples

You are called: serve again and again!
You are called as the great uplifter

The need is now where are you?

Sifting Through Time

I am in the short moments of joy and
exaltation in the time capsule of life
Picking through all the debris of life
miraculous happenings have occurred
I have pondered the positive points to
accept a flowing flag of deliberation
When I saw the *I cave* of creative
cause and existence caving in I very
carefully moved to the next *I cave*
I searched the positive plus of my life
form and will proceed intensely to
find the passage onto Eden's *Q cave*

Amalgamation in Deep Space

Trillions of light years from our
current field of vision there is life
Running in a unfathomed manner it
exists in Regeo in a different format
Initially continents do not exist and
little water remains intact only air.
Life forms drink air and feed it to all
living objects, air is the premium part
We cannot imagine this concept here
Life forms retain a different shape in
their entirety and water is used fuel
Life's compartments are carved metro
containers moving life to next steps
Surrounded by four sun stars there is
no night only everlasting day light

Awareness

I observe the glowing sunsets now
Until my eyes do fail I see richness
Through the many hues are messages
Color my life with powerful sprays
I allow the collage to penetrate life
Through all blandness I see shades
Shades of redyelloworange trickle in
They permeate my deep core inside
When life gives me black and white
I press the core and colors run wild
Often I need illumination to color
Paint the drab out of events I breathe
I must breathe colors of air and sun
Light makes me aware of fixing all
Break the darkness and filter colors
Colors will make all things bearable
I turn the many shades into serenity

Awash in Sea Water

Running with the tide has its merit
You can follow the small minnows
Sometimes see fiddler crabs dance
Then as the wash flows, a sea shell
Here I see an ancient channel whelk

Moving across the marsh: driftwood
Abundance of sea life is everywhere
An occasional jellyfish flagellates
Then a gull will crack a blue mussel
Sea water rises and teems with life

Where I see the ebb and flow occur
Creation rises and sends a message
A new day happens and there it is
Patterns emerge and there is a remap
Witness our lives are an ebb and flow

Find your ebb and flow trace patterns
Now trace your existence in the sand

Dictators Power Transfer

Orderly transition rarely occur in maniacs
They dictate until sole authority shakes
Winding down they hold on to last breath
Their farewell begins in the Adios bed

Wind Chimes are Dancing Around

There is the sound of the west wind itself
Blows unconstrained as a turbulent chime
Creating its own musical sonata of joy
Besides this pleasant whistling sublime
There are additions creating an orchestra
In the distance as I hear a soothing chime

Wind chimes all set the time they give me
a rhyme in pantomime making me climb

I will climb a hill and listen to the shrill
that allows me to fill a daffodil with skill

Wind chimes define a soothing melody
A musical tingling trilogy a repeat parody
Ending as a unique rhyme of a rhapsody

Great ringing bells mingle in the wind
reverberate and dance a powerful Spin
Tingling our skin with a single chagrin

INHERIT THE WEALTH

Often we see those waiting on fortunes
Often we observe a radical end change
Often the skylight breaks and disaster
Often events climax different expectation
Often dead men talk and leave mothballs
Often dead woman talk leave it to the cat
Often those waiting are corrupted broke
Often those waiting remain so destitute
Thenwealthgrowsinlegalbeaglecoffers

Nikos, Nikos, Nikos

We are surrounded by a victory party
Few valiantly aware it was powerful
Only those in the funeral party knew

Masses of paid hecklers and others
Those who are disinherited and lost
Mingling curiosity seekers probing
Professional agitators are abound
Weak leaders afraid of loss of power
An army of anger and confusion.

Yet for a few this is a victory march
Quietly I say NIKOS NIKOS NIKOS

While I wrestle the maddening mass
While I see the orchestrated crowd
While I see those baited with hate
While I observe a contrived ambush

Driven by the tenor of compassion
Witness the events of the lynch mob
Quietly I say NIKOS NIKOS NIKOS

Humanity shows it is manipulated
Humanity paints only todays logic
Forgetting the prophetic message
They all live in the current moment
Forgetting the word they were given
All follow the broken road ahead

I cry for their lack of understanding
I wallow in their wounded confusion
Quietly I say NIKOS NIKOS NIKOS

I observe a rising again and the tomb
I witness the empty cloth and crown
I see the heavy boulder removed
I know the reality of the resurrection
Quietly I say NIKOS NIKOS NIKOS

Calling the Great Canyon

Flow the river and see this path ahead
Have you observed the painted walls
This landscape alive with crisp hues
The earth has given us a choice gift
In response we have called it Grand
Time has created this natural uplift
Walls of carved monoliths and forms
The wandering river that flows quick
A river with a final Ocean destination
A roving river constantly bleaching
Meander a colorful mass waterway
Say to the maker it is a grand creation

Abyssinia

I observe remains of two thousand years
I search for pieces of an ancient culture
Carefully I look for signs of old mines
Finitely I explore icons of Addis Ababa

The ending reign of the Lion of Judah
Haile Salasse has finally been dethroned
The Coptic images of the street remain
No tears are shed for the Iron ruler now

Wander through the parched countryside
See Abyssinians exist with small miracles
I perceive they are so keenly industrious
Taking only what is required to survive
They are lithe and quick to live as remote

Transition yourself to the meager living
Can you live on roots and native animals
Can your shelter be rock straw and twigs
Arise and be an Abyssinian for one day

Seek the joy of East African Sun now
Somehow the parched arid desert glows
Children of the continuity they live on
Marking many conquests they survive

A Coptic priest hands to me a parchment
The writing is faint obscured and blurred
I am instructed to begin a historic search
Now I see drawings of the Covenant Ark

I search the barren caves for the ARK
After tedious days ARK remains hidden
The Ark has kept its secret cave shrouded
Abyssinians shield the codes as mystery

Abyssinia protects an Ark of the covenant
Who else remains to keep it a dire secret?

Spastic Plastic Elastics

Certain people identify with other individuals who are on the other side of far out or far cry
It is our action to be a witness to the rising creativity emerging from these unleashed minds
Perhaps we should stand and wait for genius to flow and observe the massive budding blending
Too often these created wonders are zapped we never get see the work of spastic plastic elastics

Julie Sunflower

I see the amazing flowers of life spring to a massive expanse and glow
Among the wonders I see the sunflower blossom and burst its yellow
Then there is a brown patterned center that arrays a chocolate aroma
Little Julie is observing the warmth of new life and examining a bee
Nature pollinates the radiating Sunflower that unfolds before us all
Then I know the message passed is that continuous pollination happens
I have been a witness to the miracle on new life in the garden before me
Basking in the center of life is the pollinated plants of our natural realm
I am a product of the cross pollination of life patterned in the garden
Stand up and see Julie Sunflower shine in the glow of perpetual rebirth

Our Criss-Cross Fence

I saw the true bit fence gleaming....A magnificent structure built upon
Built upon a simple side of corrals....Corrals that contain grazing cattle

A powerful crisscross design holds....Holds intact a population captive
Architecture might learn a lesson.....the simplicity of design is creative

Build me something to gaze upon....Create something of enduring value
Capture my imagination here now.....Plan simple structures to be lasting

Build a Criss Cross fence to forever

The Runners after the Race

Observe the amazing passage of the runners moving across the horizon
Multitudes pass before us as the race of life is continually unfolding
The runners pass like a furtive stampede running at full speed ahead
Perhaps there is a lesson to observe with masses of humanity charging
Are we all in the race of life that slips so quickly in front of us now?
Yet when this race is finished runners gather and celebrate completion
We pause and pose in the now and treasure our great accomplishments
We are a great mass of a maddening populace that runs the race of time
After the long and arduous race before us we continue to pace ourselves
When each race unfolds and completes we catch our breath and smile

Arise and See

Comfort is not our preordained reality
We are made as excited moving flesh
Our bodies are formed as work intent
Formed and contoured as elastic joy

Our muscle and flesh ripple to move
Shapes formed to show locomotion
Spring to unwind to lift push and pull
Spring to stretch balance and bounce

Arise and see the zest of movement
Find your best moves and then repeat
Our perfection is in the massive move
Pick a range of motion and succeed

Arise to see the magic of your moves
Arise to see a pleasant improvement
Arise and see the great development
Arise and see your body to perfection

Our protoplasm charges forward now
We begin to understand its purpose
Covering our bones and inner organs
It is the plastic that holds us together

Understand the purpose of your body
Given the gift of its beauty and boast
Use it wisely and thoroughly now
Arise and see how together you are

Challenge of the Sunrise

Today is the special morning of hope
I see a great Sun Star rise with glow
A Glow that spreads and enlightens
Go embrace the morning, Be revised
I revel in the morning light of change

Magnificent

I understand meanings of words
Several definitions fit some words
While translations are common
I find some words hard to define

Working with the experts I try
Fundamentally there is a fit
Carefully I craft a key sentence
Magnificent is excellently adorned

Perception

Our perception is at times often limited
We see only the clouded negative images
If a field of images displeases us we fret
Yet if change is possible we do very little

Open your eyes to the new panoramas
Views that are limited must be cleared
Pristine vision is necessary for decisions
Try all critical angles to achieve success

Explore and find what conforms positive
Change the old patterns of drib and drab
Clear all fields and be totally enmeshed
You are a change elixir so take charge!

Frontenac

Fierce battles took place at Frontenac
Bombardments and then mass casualties
In time Iroquois attacked the fort itself
In time the fort was overtaken enmasse
Then British wanted this wilderness fort
Then French wanted this wilderness fort
It was a bonanza sitting on the frontier
As all wars were settled then all was well
The Canadians of Canadian descent came
They settled in and took its final refuge

Finding the Footprints of Life

Struggling for a place in a civilized cage
Analysis of existence requires a footprint
Our researchers require intense details
Combing through the maze of the past
Some societies left little detail to study
Small artifacts and few traces improbable
Our mass of plastic brains will yield tons
Analysis of tons will be confusing to find
Finding chaos simple: finding order hard
They were undecided pre-blank nomads
Totally blank in detail and real purpose
Yearly they spent time reordering chaos
Tracing logical patterns was impossible
Reaching conclusions were truly simple

They spent multitudes of time amusing
They spent significant minutes confusing
They ran out of hours to really stabilize
They spent too many days to mobilize
In the end they drifted to a destabilize
Times sand glass made them synchronize

Mechanical people fail to act we know
Societies which fail to act will just creak

Allagash Wilderness

Slowly floating down ancient rivers
Guides become necessary to adjust
Several people have been lost here
Wilderness in a foreign place for man
Repeat travelers understand the wild
It becomes easy to become confused
Rooted scenery all looks the same ahead
Astute path finders are aware of change
Minor changes in the landscape noted
Trailblazers know all rock tree and plant
Search the countryside for continuity
Everything flows together and repeats
Our life blood and existence a challenge
Trace your new flow line in the Allagash
Understand you are strangers always
Find an everlasting guide to Forever Mtn
Your journey requires massive assistance
The canoe ready.... choose your life guide
Push forward for the river bound journey

Encounter on the First Bridges

I understand what we were taught
History was written with all positive
When the first shot was fired...chaos
Chaos ensued and the enemy stood
Panic prevailed amongst the troops
This was not suppose to happen here
It was the shot heard round the world
Remember dead at Lexington Green
Who are the fallen at Concord Bridge
Do I know their names and family
Do I see their cause as a just one
Am I aware of all the details there
Did they bring unity and Patriotism
Well it is our job to preserve freedom
We may only be aware of its ideal
Paul Revere got as far as Cambridge
William Dawes reached Lexington
Sam Prescott got to Concord Bridge
He was the the one who warned them
Sentries were amassed in Cambridge
Have you got further than Cambridge

Accept Your Role and Reel forward

Often we become inundated with details
We become overwhelmed in our midst
Our life action requires real movement
The load we carry now must be lifted
Arise and be accounted in the masses
We are an alternative strength of the ages
Be lifted in your roles and command all
Command your future moving forward
Reel in the power and recharge your day
Take action and revitalize your future

PASS ON PLAY

Species Dream

Now a fossil in time turns up
Now the ancient form revealed
Was the dream to progenate
Was it powering to superiority
Unaware it became frozen image
A tremendous being it was but failed to amass grow
Numbers are the key to success to become a scale
Scale to a fast population that becomes the Power
Power spreads and reigns supreme and finally ebbs
Once upon a Cryptosaurus a terrifying reign ensued
Suddenly a cataclysm occurred then massive die off.

PRY OPEN THE CAN OF COMPLEXITY

FIND THE KEYNOTE OF YOUTH
THRIVE IN THE MESSAGE GIVEN
WE LEARN QUICKLY OR PERISH
LITTLE TIME REMAINS TO BE IDLE
BE A VICTOR IN THE RACE OF TIME
THE VALVE OF EXISTENCE POURS ON
SURE OPENINGS
OPENINGS ARE MANY AND EVOLVE TO COMPLEXITY
PRY OPEN THE VALVE AND LOCATE PEACE PASSAGE
PEACE PASSAGE IS ENTERED BY THOSE WHO GIVE IT
LOCATE YOUR GROWING PASSAGE WITH TIME TICKING
CHOSE THE FLAGGING ENTRANCE AT SERENITY DOOR

Connect the Passage

Traverse the rounded mountain pass
around the bend a massive herd I see

As far as I observe thousands of animals
A massing of Bison on the great plains
We can only imagine this point in time

Now we only focus on rotting carcasses
Our abundance was squandered by GG
GG slaughtered for the sport and surge

We are still slaughtering in a like manner
This time they squeeze the trigger on us

Provide To The Masses-Light

They are finding difficulty here
I see that they graze and observe
Often they believe what is printed
Often they fail to test the words
Often they fail to filter the media
Paragraphs pounce on pendulums
Paragraphs swing things and blur
Paragraphs create cohesive crisis
Sentences slice through the mice
Sentences wave through the rave
Sentences behave to make a slave
Words imprint indelible thoughts
Words flow like raging rivers
Words flow and roll uncontrolled
You believed what was told to you
You were molded into a package
You were blown over in trusting
Remember everything an opinion
Remember hardly any real facts
Remember the hearsay and buzz

Tomorrow wake up to test all of it
You were programmed in darkness
Open the VISTA window to think
Allow masses of light penetration
I am feeding you masses of light
Prepare yourself for one newthink
Lines of rays filter the truth intact
Locate the lines of persistent light
See how thoughts can be reformed
Open! - I provide the masses light

LIGHT THE FIRE IN FORCE

I once became a frozen cold statue
Times were brutal snow and winds
Piling over the snow drifts a worry
Quickly you could be buried alive
Now I need a crested Flag of Hope
Locate me to a cave in Cremona

My hope is on the backside light
Array me in the forest so unaware
Present me to the master open pit
Assist my effort in getting to light
Massive fiery lumens erase dark
Massive lumens fire rays of light
New flames inspire our intellect

Spread the warmth of brilliance
Then power the Fire in brilliance

Taking the business by firestorm
Locate the new waves of flame
I am all about to celebrate melting
Time has been our friend at last
March to the sanity shuffle of trees
When spring returns in I say ready

Roll a light source into truth now
We are pioneers running forward
Arise move forward with a lantern
Set your lantern of learning high
Angle forward with words now
Teach all compatriots knowledge

The fire of truth rests in learning
Find out figure out or be left out

Weather Patterns a Change

While I dreamed all was together firmly
Suddenly patterns in the weather changed
Catastrophic undercurrent was occurring
This reforming wave of weather hit quick
We cannot slow the power of nature at all
I become a victim of nasty rain clouds
Yet every day created has a personality
We must endure the driving rain storm
Water showers washed and rinsed clear
Our new day is ozone clear and mellow

I Massed Over the Walls of Exclusion

They put up barriers and isolated me
I was not hurt by their futile actions
Pile driving forward I felt total release
Their containment captured their egos

Ancient barrels of fermented prune juice
Marching in the parade of pinhead pride
They slipped and ingested prune paste
Since they needed a total cleaning out
Their precision was exact and quick
They ran well into the majestic toilets
Their attitudes were flushed to moon isle

Today I see their pruned ideas growing
Barriers that isolated me are decaying
I arrived to the top of Stuck up mountain
When the prune army arose in regalia
They displayed their purple perplexity

Now I see the brittle buns of bellicose
Now I rest in the slippery mud Mounds
The end result of exclusion was putrid
March out of the walls of exclusion
March back to the castle of containment
Start it all over again...egos never fade

Rising Quickly

I need to foresee the mass of needs here
I need to feel the emptiness of without
When the cry of compromise is heard
I will arise quickly and note changes
I will arise and brace myself for revision

There are no real heroes that come
forward Empty minds never fill the voids
created I must move onward and be the
candidate There is a lack of unity and real
purpose I see that cohesiveness is now
the answer

I must arise and ameliorate the situation
I must arise to be an instrument of change
I must arise and be heard in the assembly
I must arise and be the key unifying force
I must arise and become the real solution
I must arise and quickly fill up this void

Waving the Great American Standard

Charge to the patriotic music blending
March to the spangled trumpet tune
Listen to the unison of melodies that play
In the distance beats of the music heard
The harmonious magic tune settles inside
You have risen to the nationalistic chorus
Play these tunes in your head and blare
You become the standard to all the notes

Soaring on the High Thermals

Soaring with the Condors... there is a possibility to glide to new vistas
Remembering that they were transplanted then we do accommodate it
Riding the high thermals of life we prepare to make many adjustments
Rising to the mission of new hope and challenge we remain intact now
Yet a forward call of lifes journey will pull us out of comfort routines
All zones we know to exist will morph and rapidly realign to future IO
Our eventual understanding will map forward to a revision Road ahead
Future IO will design a reticent road ahead that calls us to amazement
Amazement is our focus.. we begin to understand how to ride thermals
Thermals : our keynote tracing our future events with new perspective

Finding Great Ideas to Use

I am so independent at times my brainstorms become ready made hash ideas I utilize to survive from one day to the next
Yet I clearly understand that My ideas are not clear and precise going forward in time I must modify these seeds to survive
My seed mix will change and be rearranged to emphasize great vintage ideas accepted and restated to meet todays need
I will follow the compass path of truth and build a bridge of transition to arrive at New Brainstorm over a Great Flow river

Keeping the Ready House

There is something inside all of us that remains adamant about certain aspects of life that should remain in constancy
Perhaps this is an acceptable premise that we retain certain character traits learned and accepted early in the ready house
Arise now and allow the floodgates of change to open wide and create a place for new ideas to enter your heart and soul
Will I find you in the ready house constructing these rampant ideas getting a treatise prepared to assist others in transition
Will I find you leading the revision charge of massive renewal as many programs are changing and some are fading fast
Will I find the rapid movement of civilization race so quickly that the pace is too rapid for the great multitudes to catch
Will I see the illumination of your heart being a beacon of compassion to those who struggle daily to locate Sanity Street
Will I arise in the middle of the night to assist you in your dire sickness agonizing through everything to remain alive now
Should you fail to really understand how to keep a ready house you will wallow in massive marshmallow inaction forever

Seeking Northern California

How the Sea Lions rule

I see how ferocious they are in their group and understand their power of hierarchy
Only one is in charge and everyone comes to know their place in the group matrix
Very few challenges are made since the massive prince of the pod shows raw power
When threats are made there is need to be a structure of precision and real defense
Waddling there is no place for laggards in a pod:order needed and places to survive
Locate a sea lion order chart and begin analyzing your place in the human structure
All societies have rules of order and action : See your face in a multitude of crowds

Trekking Across the great New Habitat

Finding a pathway becomes a creative wandering through tall brush, retaining your own trail to follow, do not be overcome by nature
Bustling around the corners we see more ground needed to be covered and successfully conquered to maintain an existing habitat
Significant masses are concerned that the watering down of the republic will bring the unordered chaos that suffocates our great hope
In the many tomorrows rising on the planet a deliverance seems to be a recalcitrant possibility to render we the people a voice of light
See how those enlightened signposts can electrify your vision : You are now living in a captivated New Era : Mingle your voice strong

Declaring our Rights to Change and Rearrange
We believe our personal rights trump any degree of our opening ourselves to what humanity labels mass responsibility
Total Americanism is buried in a morass about rights and rights and more rights creating a red flare of indelible idiocy
Can we continue to rise without a check of sanity? Can we continue to declare compassion for crommbow caterpillars?
Do we perceive that there are intelligent limits to the declared rights of the multitudes of starving shalargo sting sharks?
Are we immune to the mass migration of wildebeast in East Africa should we build them a superhighway to a Serengeti?
Can we somehow cope with the wounded Chipmunks of Chippewa? Can they get precision medical care in Patchawawa?
Allow your heart to sink into a mass disposal of human babies smoldering in the huge dump site at Boston City Hospital.

Washed at the Columbia River Gorge

A massive stretch along the mighty Columbia is fed by the side waters
Rushing streams and brooks cut through underbrush to refresh a river
Rolling waters cascade off sides of shear rock facings as thundering falls
Our minds try to comprehend volumes of natures gift waters descending
We are receivers of great water refreshers quenching our continual needs
In a grand swath of the Columbia a magical memory retains it promise
A might of rivers depend on the continual feeders that wash them clean
A power of rivers is retained in rills that feed them on a spoken journey
Columbia Power is in a gorge of wonder with cascading residual beauty

Umpqua Light to Guide You

In the bleak darkness of the Oregon coast mired with real contentious fog
Constantly sailors look in a distance for markers to guide them from shore
On thick pea soup nights fog horns blare to allow others to know positions
It becomes a Sea symphony of music on the Oregon coast and all listen
From the shore Umpqua Lighthouse operates at a sure marine steadiness
Assist the mariners searching for a pathway through natures dense mass
We are all but challenged oarsmen searching for natures landing place
Umpqua Light beams as a haven of hope for groping sailors searching
A lighthouse painted several times over as the master of the Oregon Coast
We get our sea bearings as our flotilla moves cautiously and carefully now

All Rocks at Crescent City

There are boulders of belief to protect us from rages of a New Tsunami
Even breakwaters as powerful as Bastille to stifle rising ocean currents
Then we use a seawall to stall: a protective dike to stop waters invasion
Many rocks are repositioned to hold the Pacific in its natural cradled crib
Yet the ferocious wind and powerful currents slam into the Grand Ocean
So a Pacific becomes a frenzied mass murderer of sorts come thrashing
Whipping along in a below sea level mode tracing to a Tsunami tenacity
A coastline will be attacked at dawn yielding to a powerful storm now
All rock structures needed to protect wounded humanity vying to survive

Calls from Our Trenches

Pain can afflict us very suddenly
In the past we have been stunned
Mighty afflictions rise rapidly
We yelp as Sea Dogs in our pain
In many instances remain tranced
There are no cures for upandidas
We must bask in the rays quickly
Hope we have a mild case of tarkis
Walking through life on orange bo
Move to the front to declare war.
Trench alertness maintains quiet
Observe all star-studded loses now
Go to the tank straits and revel to
Revel to a forgotten March debris
We are a tool of two solidarities
Come announce our dual escape
We are rite brimadoons rising so
Our trenches activate capillaries
Bleeding we are still in resistance
Our capitan declares invincibility
Trenches will bleed until last drops
Carry all upandidas bodies onward
We are the stop gap gate guardians
Should we fail all crash basswards
All trenches drench to hemoglobin
Thanks for the memories Mr Death

Marathon 2013

Time did catch up to us here enmasse
A swing song of our run was impasse
We had great elements surrounding
We arose on a trail of feet pounding
t could not have been a better day
Knowing all hills and heights in array
We measured the trail yet so precisely
Success now appears to be concisely
Flying low became our real dream
All camaraderie is here to redeem
Riding the pack became our theme

Running in clusters our strategy feeds
t is in our knowledge to test speeds
Reflect capabilities of former races
Running now at a cadence of paces
Our end outcomes may be forecasted
Fleetness is our motto now podcasted
Our happiness a wild cheering crowd
We run in a magnificent pack so loud
Wind a trail rippling in unison grown
Our place in the pack of life is known

Suddenly we hear crashing cymbals
Yet not the kind from joyous hymnals
Cymbals collide to more due quaking

Ground quakes many blocks shaking
Time not a consideration : only finish
Grounds quake twice now to diminish
Music does not play a pleasant hymn
Fireballs fail to play at times anthem
We hear chaotic tunes past April noon
Runners are diverted to end dirt soon
The Finish line became a ruined dune
Diversion unknown places out of tune

Goals were changed and rearranged
Life became a huge clock deranged
Time stopped here at twofifty o'clock
For we all are now in a state of shock
Time cannot run backwards to replace
Our friends were lost a huge misplace
We cannot hug them a small embrace
Tomorrow we hear a whirr : a drum
Then heartbreaking strings that strum
All Boston has reflected feeling numb

Canto of Lost Music

Strains of the symphonic rises aglow
My background begins a quiet flow
I hear this melody of continuity slow
Notes from instruments begin to grow
Over and over a piece repeats a bow
Imbedded in my brain as I now know
A canto of lost music will soon show
I will translate the sounds in one row
Repetition in my head falls like snow
I find this critical so I write to endow
Generations gather so anxious in tow
Lost music found is gold like mellow
Play a canto to the moon in afterglow

Plying My Best Words Forward

Crinkle is my least known used word
It flaps its wings an exotic rare bird
Massive my favorite overused word
Too big to fit into a corral with a herd
I chase many words like an albatross
To find I am grounded in super gloss
I start over with a word for redundant
Then find its use cannot be abundant

Often I run to check my old thesaurus
Finding no substitute for stegosaurus
So I am happy to announce a T phone
In twenty years it will be so unknown
Practice is a word that is so physical
Seven years to figure I am whimsical
Tomorrow I rise and become aligned
Escape is a word that will get unbind
When I use words like good measure
That is when I find my true treasure

Ply my by words as a regal doubloon
Hope they flow or they speak buffoon
I take my comfort in early afternoons
When I rise I inflate sixtysix balloons
Cruiser is a river word I so often use
Cantilever I chose at bridges I peruse
Flight has a unique word called lift
Without any oars at sea we are adrift
Find a right word that describes need
Tomorrow I award you a golden reed

CHAOS

There are no words to describe a Chaos
When an event goes awry its unplayos
We cannot judge what is to be normal
Perhaps it is a suit and tie semi-formal
Then again as river presses to over flow
Water will break the dam a major blow
Crashing down upon the village below
As a majestic race horse gallops ker pow

All the world is radical one raving rages
Yell and scream as if they were in cages
Get attention they arrive late to detention
Speaking very loud they seek an attention
Ranting and reeling they desire a mention
Even so their name associates to tension
Ride the wild boar through a quiet store
So I will now try my chaos all the more

Locate and find an semblance of order It
may be north or south of the border
Messages pass under the narrow door
Could chaos happen close as next store
Waving and screaming blood is streaming
I clearly see it happen I am not dreaming
Anger and passion may lead to an assault
Clearly in denial when it is not my fault

I will arise eagerly to see what is my role
Place all my compassion at a water hole
Help wounded recover clean and sterile
Patch all dressings keep them from peril
Pounding the camp we need to keep low
Courage and fortitude is what I show
My action is to reflect my great resistance

A Flash Across Erin

Mass Across a Green Island

Walking on a street in Kildare near a thatched roof house I came across a bus beckoning me across a green island Eden
Gradually as the bus began its winding course I began to think of why I was here in the first place and second place now
As the bus trek travelled I remembered a huge edifice called the Rock of Cashel where ancient Kings ruled the land mass
Then I recalled a bridge called Three Penny and thought it was outrageous to charge poor people to walk across its span
This bridge was a great inspiration along with a place entitled Knock where a rainbow said knock before entering heaven

Glendalough

I see this tower rising
It is an escape hatch
Let marauders leave
The design has power
Vikings are busy now
Yet many slow movers
They were slaughtered
These casualties buried
Once all signals clear

We begin to retrace life into the abbey to convert Erin
Once again we slowly raise our natives and pacify raiders
While Raider parties continue..Saint Kevin's tower stands
One day Brian Boru will drive V raiders out permanently
So walk across a field in peace and observe emerald shine
See it shine to a glossy green pea fog that slowly settles

Celtic tower stands create wild Viking bands on our lands
Glendalough remains in hands to allow for spiritual plans
Pouring out a spirit in strands create mass lustre grands
Memory blands deliver high demands into Erin's uplands
Ply on the lowland sands to make several sea fog stands
Upright plans delve into detail wands across multi clans

Glendalough lands remain to stand sky pointed strands

Charcoals Remain

Continually across an Irish coast wild heathens attack thatch
Cottages are burned many times to challenge all authorities
Poor farmers often burned cottages out with smoldering peat
Once the Irish are declared free Thatch smolders into disuse

On the West Coast Of Eire

Challenging coastal rises and troughs create a contrast
Often in the bright afternoon sun I can see elves align
This mystical land is capable of hiding fireflies in bogs
Certain angling rays of light can delight our vision field
Once upon a whistling night storm mounded graves open
Paralyzing the countryside with ghostly vertical visions
Then I saw a butterfly with a net chase a man as a catch
Just then Rhododendrons pinked the countryside highhills
Then I see leprechauns carefully create a mystical magic
Suddenly I awoke from my dream to see a road washout
My bus left for the train station rolling without wheels
My brain must congeal..Did this truly happen in Galway?

See Celtic Crosses at
Rock of Cashel
Heights
Brave souls await
Is there another stop
The destination reign
We are on high here?
Someone shouts no
Therefore we must go
Action awaits a revival arrival for an exclusive you
High hills are not Heaven but merely a holding point
Arise now and continue past celtic crosses abounded
Your detail journey ascends to unending skies to fly

Mark the Masses Moving to Mystical Madness

Yesterday I witnessed the flow of lost people running toward the tunnel of transition at a maddening pace for analysis
Before me I configured a herd mentality galloping toward the edge of the plateau seeking massive mystical mendacity
Could this be the next thrill over the hill that I was seeing and reporting or was it the new safety in numbers syndrome
Great masses of humanity are running on empty seeking a revised plan to rejuvenate themselves for next week or after
The herd moves with the advice of the next mystical spokesperson awaiting to transform your life to new beginnings
Arise now and see through the bland elevated hypocrisy You are now in need of a guide with a guidebook of real clarity
Arise and wash yourself in the Jordan River a profound healing is needed to re map life onto a rocky Emmaus road ahead

Trudging Through the Corridors of Crisis

Have you been put on the spot and blasted with complaints and ear buzz
Falling from the safety nets of New Neuroses are Merry Murky Mouths
We see they continually work a populace on extreme needs and wants
We have been inundated with a pampered mass of we deserve it requests
However now earthquakes of awake has hit us with tremendous tremors
The entitled generation has arrived for the rude reawakening ceremonies
Great trumpets will role out our themes of heavy saddened songs of woe
Drifting music will catapult a notion that change may permeate the air
Our Republic engine can take only twelve carloads of disenchantments
Await an arrival of a conniver caboose we see insidious sentinels remain

Ignite the Fires of Reality

We are aware we live in reverberating bubbles of best guess in solving
Solutions are forthcoming to answer many puzzles that bind us severely
Answers do not arrive promptly only shrieking gets attention deservedly
Many critical problems delay and decay until an emergency horn sounds
Fires burn brightly yet no attention is focused on the accumulate dangers
Our society only responds to the aftermath wreckage massed on 2 tracks
Wake up and deliver a bellicose answer that falls upon wedged eardrums
The fires of reality are ignited at night for all to observe clearly concise
Reality lights a continuous pattern written in a finite evening sky now
We the people are immune to raging political fires that will consume us

Seek the Vermillion Hills

My vision paints a vermillion canvas before me that transforms my self
I am propelled to take the brush strokes and color my many horizons
I must move quickly and concisely to see sun rays down on quiet hills
Great Kaibab uplifts of Scarlet brown and miraculously Mirror red now
All shadows move to recreate a perfect painting of Kaibab sandstone
Arrive at the scene of massive beauty and revel in its majestic red tones
I am the observers of fine lines of crested beauty guided by my hands
I can paint the images of what I see on the plain canvas before myself
Yet I cannot create the vermillion hills that were formed by times hand

FIND THE RIGHT COMBINATION TO CREATE AND LIVE A DREAM

Slowly and precisely I will take action to begin my creative vision
Often I have thought this dream but now I must begin to live a dream
Time has flowed through the message machine and the sand is gone
A call to reality requires a commitment to creativity and good balance
Measure the days ahead and allow for bites of time to think and create
Since the hourglass of time has run new strategies will be appearing
For I am About leveling a new agenda I am about finding the words
Tomorrow and more tomorrows color my majestic word projections
My creation must climb to the seat of new vision and communicate
Time flows with powerful and promising volumes...execute the days!

Valley of Tenuous Trumpets

While many are in the mode of suffering....a helping hand will wave the signals of hope and assurance despite the pains
Walls of indifference cover our hearts .. I see myself being a partial paratrooper of peace and assistance in many situations
Rise I hear and cover the landscape with a promise of change....help is in our hearts with the government its only numbers
When I hear a great roll of trumpets and brass my action cannot be tenuous... an active corp of crusaders must be affirmed

Finding Our Heartbeat

We toil and work in a time of great transition and turmoil as populations pulsate for Freedom and more Freedom
Thus we are overseers of the great passion for a clear breath of good air without being enchained in tribal jails
Our heartbeat reverberates for the masses that are held back in the dogma of massive control and captivation
Understand and be compassionate then allow your heartbeat to roll a drumbeat for freedom.. freedom.. freedom

Probing the Mass Messages Catapulting

I meander through the words of hundreds of people trying to influence every precise move I make how cunning they are

They are wise umbriargos who calculate the moment of times execution waiting my move
I must delete the messages of the hundreds who invade my quiet personal beach head now
I will secure my place and rivet my energy to do wise and productive actions in my life
Charging from the house I see the inane and insane movements of those compromising
Focusing I realize I have no time for rancid opinions and mediocre plans for destruction
I will therefore arise and amend the morning and delete the decay from my open screen
Conclusions mandate that I must justify my clear cut actions before Armageddon begins
The mass messages of great understanding will promulgate the day as a catapult delivering
Ready yourself for the total blaze of truth to penetrate your eardrums and roll forever!

Filtering the Words Coming from the Countryside

Hearing messages of mass chaos and death rings through my total being concern to alarm Culture is going mad....
We have created a mass culture of death words from those are plugged in the at the top..Their reaction is null and void
How can the leadership be so evasive and numb to the culture we have designed now   Where is their openness to wisdom
Observe now carefully we have papered and painted so that ..... intolerable Madness will prevail across the countryside....
We will suffer the matter heavily until we observe a swing song of mass bleeding empowers someone to shout RESTART

Finding Our Life Passion

Overcoming my fears
quickly I march onward
Bared closely by those in
command I slowly watch
In my passion to be right
Painstakingly I move over the mountains of concern
My thoughts drive me to question my planned path
Who can lead me to be the smartest new solution
Yea I must form my dialogue to meet my passion
Fear a state I must be beyond Defend Stand in battle!

CHARM MY LISTENING AUDIENCE

Walking on eggshells is not an imperial action or reaction
Be yourself and be accepted for your new gifts and talents
Walk slowly to arise and merge yourself into a persona
Hold yourself carefully and collectively to a new standard
You may be the powerful thought moving across the land
Arise and grow your words and mold them so powerfully
At a certain time you may move mountains stone by stone
Chart yourself forward with major optimism you will grow
Plant your seeds of optimum in the furrows of a fanaticism
Uniquely your gifts and my gifts can setup a new bonfire
Move ahead with a persona for truth and compassion now
A empty train must be filled with great thoughts and action
Move as express trains in massive missions of deliverance

My Doll Rosie

I see our Jacque clutching her doll
This a picture of true compassion
If we cannot hug a doll then what
We become a mechanical society
Living becomes an mild gesture
Humanity is a robotic experience
The crowd of mad maniacs is void
Our life experience is a small hug
I need to demonstrate real caring
Can a child teach us a lesson here
The pride of keeping all in order
The show of love in beamed faces
An outward patience and calm
See how we should act in the now
A child's face can measure it all
Transform your thoughts to peace
Take ownership of life experience
We are all in the one ship moving
Keep Rosie happy with kindness
Care about all the small matters

Mountain Laurel

Coming in March Mountain laurel
See branches as drooping masses
Masses of Lavender blossoming
Everywhere vigorous overlays are
I see Phoenician Purple coloring
Overwhelmed in the magnificent
The blossoms give us grape aroma
The smell permeates the country
Everywhere Mountain Laurel rises
Here great Texas Mountain Laurel
Now waves its branches in the sun
Alive Laurel presents tiny clusters
For only a short season lifes hues
I think I will paint it in my dreams
Remembering a clear picture beam
A wind gust allows it to be a wave
Yes allow violet masses to tingle
If they were bells they will signal
Yes send a signal of springs arrival
Announce the purple day enmasse

Finding Cibola

It is my desire to uncover Cibola
Passionately I search with verve
I may be on great discovery trails
Yet the vision I have is to map all
Finding Cibola can be challenging
Ergo I cannot stop this old passion
Continually I am possessed now
Rolling forward I will chart a path
Charging into I will see a pinpoint
Tracing all known facts to locate it
Step by step I see seven pinpoints
There can be only one conclusion
Seven Cities are there but hidden
My role is to find all seven cities
My map maker has assured me yes
In a tedious study I carefully see
City of Blanco, Sentata, LosViejo,
Mas Grande, El Gato, Nueva Rojo
and Rio Bonita are real places, See
My hope:Cibola es con mucho oro

23

Flow with the river of life

I have been immersed in the running river of life and I am ecstatically overjoyed
Oh how the flow of the river carries me to unknown destinations I am unfamiliar
Time will settle me but I rebel vociferously at the these new places and new faces
Suddenly this river of life takes me to its origins where I realize that I am reformed

Mesas and Buttes Abound

Of all the forms and shapes that enter a landscape of my mind I find this
Massive Vermillion rocks color the canyons of my multitudinal thoughts
For miles and miles in the caverns of my brain I see Mesas and Buttes
Perhaps it is the Grand Canyon images that I carry and cannot let go
Then perhaps it is the Arizona Vistas that permeate my deep trenches
This I know that I simply cannot let go of the many vermillion shapes
Massive domed structures have entered the crevices of my cranium now
These redorangebrown creations have given me a grand uplift to heaven
My life has become a panorama of natures finest castles and cathedrals
I see the high desert features that even the artist cannot duplicate in time

Spray the Subject

See how the fun begins when the spray node hose is now pointed at you
The spray of refreshing water will wake you to the water funnels of life
He who holds the hose controls the focused spray mist that drizzles now
While the gardens and fruit trees need water feeding sprays abound here
Laughing hoses clearly give me a smiling cheer of approval and fill me
Be prepared to be dampened by water trajectories that have been aimed
You are a target of the mischief that surrounds you so get ready for mist
Drifting mists will slowly baptize your total being and cool you down
Be ready for an excitement bath for you now are chosen amongst many

Intricacies

Climbing the hill to the very top is similar to a visit to a special A shrine
I traverse the trail that slowly winds to the apex of the mountain above
I know that on top will give me a new up view of the Arizona landscape
So I begin my journey and have great hope in a futuristic evolving vision
How will I enjoy the precipice and looking down upon a valley of Sun?
Rocks and boulders surround narrow points at the pinnacle of promise
Their sharp edges provide a notice that everything is not so perfect now
I will arise with the knowledge my imperfection and not dwell upon it
I will venture from this pinnacle of intricacies then decide on changes
The intricacies of revision will begin with me and then project forward

Parallel IO Code

Generations move in concise code
Communication proceeds motion
All participants listen very closely
Hearing is in the verbal instruction
Word is not wasted in deep space
IO codes are presented to follow
One mistake in the IO command
Then your Space Vehicle disables
No finite fix or repair is possible
Your fate is frozen in light years
Majestic Z's appear on IO boards
Missing vehicles drown in capsule
Z marks our time space graveyard
Correct IO codes become essential

Climbing the Ladder

We simply slip in our quick trips
Once we try to fix all the glicks
Then we realize how to mix pick
Our failure was to click the nicks
When the hicks kick the wicks
Torn free it is impossible to relick
Find the slick rungs and begin fix
We are about to re stick the crick
Then we can mend a flick trick
Shimming we tick the slick stick
We should have used a few bricks!

Magnanimous Mentality

Few souls know the needs of others
Too often I am too about me content
Select people of adverse experience
They sense the dire forgotten needs
Traveling across the momentum sky
Traveling through the briar brush
Immediately they pick up on dull pain
Perception mandates quick action
Chosen me diaries are visionaries
Traveling through many trellises
Sparks are aglow and now assistance
They do not wait for others action
Magnanimous action is soon abound
Mentality arises to mend the hurt
Now this is the action of real Saints
Arise and wash the wounded lepers!

Enter Centos Quantos

I will envision the future of my
families families families future
Should families exist on our planet
Going onward my spirit will allow
I somehow allow for acceptance
Whatever acceptance evolves to
Should societal breakdown erode
Then the city state will direct you
You will be instructed how to live
You are instructed who will live
I reject control but am powerless
Your future may be decided ahead
Enter the Centos Quantos factor

Presiding over Anger

Many times I am freely challenged
My compatriots are competitive
In a midst they push me to a line
Their action creates severe anger
Groups prod single wound results
I see the group mentality justified
No one takes issue for our wound
Pushing the envelope whistle clean
I am angered over the blank group
Someday each to face their match
Meanwhile my end stop will clear
In the prevailing dust they will fall
My anger needs to quell with time
Future Images will unravel groups
I need to heal my brain wound
Pride can crush my unstitch bones

Finding the Heart of Life

My true meaning and purpose is
I propose that it is initially hidden
I discover my key attribute buried
Knowing this it remains covered
I come dashing out when needed
Once I am discovered it will ring
People will know me more then
Yet the Heart of Life develops
When attributes are identified
I then must relinquish my cave
Open to the Heart of life flowing
Communicate my power purpose

Massive Charging Lobos

The pack comes swiftly to destroy
Unaware I now stand in the pathway
My senses have telegraphed a danger
The quiet of the countryside known
Known since all other wildlife serene
Charge forward be on a set defensive
The pack is poised to vicious attacks
Massive blood curdling howls prevail
Alpha pack lead is a death architect
Profound head has a survival instinct
Defending perimeters are critical
Profound courage requires firmness
Staying power will succeed in time
The Lobo lunge comes to slay us
Now I am ready and will overcome
Packs come so I will stand in victory
No longer fearing I am well prepared
Alpha Lead comes to be soon slayed
Sentry spears and sharpened knives
Out of sheaths the defense will rise
I cut down Lobo forces of death now
Slashing bloodied snow remains now
I have overcome the death knell now
Today I will declare victory in Vernal
Tomorrow I will celebrate uprisings
I quelled lobos using noxious ploys
Uprisings are neutralized patiently
Unwind the charge of death slowly
Our mission is to corral the leaders
Contain charging Lobos in lock step
Freedoms plan constant containment
Lobos are the harassment to contain
End the reign of fury with loves spear

THE BRIDGE ADJOINING

Connect the joy of life with bridges
Observe all the seen inter connects
No longer are we land lock in cabins
We are located in the Kauszameld
Our mission to travel to Parosatown

We are given an ultimatum to join
Our bridge takes us across waters
We are thinking of getting on a path
See the bridge adjoining we are ready
Fast moving nights gallop to infinity

Now there is passage over calm river
Bridges will save you when it rages

Growing New Lives

I see how we have influence in the now
Our thoughts may be transmitted forward
Our children sometimes listen in part
I understand their reasons : wisdom waits
When solutions are sought lights aglow
The kernel of truth pops when fired up

We cannot have immediate control here
New generations must arise and be heard
Relative truth is awash in complications
Real truth marches beyond expectation
The flow of Generation ZYX is profound
Alliances will lead them to the core truths

Locate a banner of wisdom tree growing
Words and actions communicate truth
Find your part and deliver the statements
Growing forward is not terrestrial wonder
Passion to take a next correct action now
Find peace under wisdom tree branches

Giving of Ourselves

My personal vision is about this me
What I see I am doing with my life
Others perceive a self derivation null
Participate in a grand march is well
Yet I have adorn myself with confetti
I celebrate the great me in one style
There is little room for other voices

Then when drums beat I am alone
I march to the tune of indifference
Participating was not in our pet plans
Once the parade music stops we fold
Our outline ended some friend glared
As loners we are unhappy B- players
Then new music chimes in a distance

Find the handle of self-giving in life
Pride is a dead word buried in sorrow
Life flows to those who participate in
Hearing the new chimes breathes now
Locate the new you in a whirring note
Play a plain symphony of self-giving
A crown of peace and patience awaits

Climb to a Spirit of Mass Renewal

Lacking a defined trail I must now renew
Contours on the landscape may devastate
I must locate the slipping points walking
My mission continues to be a challenge
Finding myself lost several times rethink
Rethinking is a boon to stop and consider
My life is a steady jaunt: a forward climb
My destination a mountain:Mass renewal

Racing Full Speed

Can my speed be controlled by signs
Maybe it is controlled by speed traps
Should it be stopped by trees or poles
Perhaps stone walls will slow it down
Then friend John B hit a car pile up
Racing at full speed can be real fatal
Lewis hit the HI Speedy Pizza sign
My friend was only driving at 125
My friend bled to death on the Artery
I could not ask him what happened
All blood and bits on Southern Artery
Other remains to squeegees on a mop

My Garden Grows and Flows

So this is the time to plant and sow
Tomorrows abundance relies on now
Yes I plant in September in Arizona
Surely once a flow of heat dissipates
Excitedly I run to grab a hoe to sow
My feet trickle down paths with seeds
Opening seed packets to space seeds
Slowly seeds drop to be hoe covered
The land is groomed and anointed
Reminder sticks cut to empty packets
Waters of life will flow on fertile land
Plant food falls into all tiny furrows
After many tomorrows I will perceive
Growth can spring in winter gardens

Charging Great Sandstone Buttes

With great excitement I climb upward
Challenges change my physiognomy
Quickly I race to a mounted uprise
My form assumes a sure footed ram
Scrambling I continually race up up
There remains many rising buttes
Climbing I observe several vistas
Sometimes I slip on the sandstone
The soft earth crumbles at my feet

Now I call out to the Sonora desert
Rescue me as a wild charging ram
I am transformed to my surroundings
Help me acclimate my restless mind
Allow me the peace of a desert wind
Reform my anxious self to a serenity
Find the wild streak I have acquired
Tame my aggressive spirit now alive
Allow me to flow as a peaceful river
Flow me to quiet place to meditate
Power my creativity to a still moment
Quiet is a place of my transformation

Meteor Showers shadow our lives

Massive space particles cloud me out
My vision is obscured rising ahead
Amazed I perceive huge open space
The space debris culminates out here
I am bombarded with finite pieces
Continually I see sky hawk on fire
Skyhawk dances in upper atmosphere
They roll across my celestial sphere
At a maddening pace they fill my sky

Often Perseids give me annual shows
Sometimes I stay awake to observe
It reminds me of broken pieces I see
My life has shed finite particles now
Across an open sphere of me : Chaos
As I wonder often I emit my particles
Filling the void of time with troubles
Soon I will pass through an open sky
In a self propulsion my showers end

Having been Aptly Chosen

No one person will commit to key tasks
Failure is not an widely approved agenda
Since no one would march ahead blindly
Therefore I chose me to tackle three tasks
Cranking in a quick pace... lights went on
Then in the forward corner see a solution
Initially young children volunteer a work
Young children act and do all the set up
Then the backdrops need attention here
Hence the young adults do good props
Young adults are advanced and elected
Then the mature members cry foul here
Whence the elder propellers arise again
Mature masses sell ideas-tickets-venues
I was aptly chosen to be the paste master!

My SCHEDULE

What is SCHEDULE for each of us?
Personally my layout has not worked
My schedule : a target for interruption
All the mighty mercenaries attack me
A defined purpose of order : realigned
Patiently I spent time to juggle it all
Then a Grand Master Menace arrived
This Grand Master wants top priority
Now I arrive back at tickety tock time
Caving in was not in my daily flow
Master Menace has tic power to wield
Tic power can vaporize my life plan
Now I cave in and allow for Menace
So I massage todays plan schedule
Tomorrow my challenge: Fit it all in

A New Rising is Coming

Change is Rearranging our Lives

Observe how the masses are worked over and moved by boatloads of false staged compassion to change and rearrange
Our lives are manipulated by the galvanized gorillas that push their agenda upon the masses to the satisfaction of a few
Galloping herds of wild horses are coming to trample to erase sensations of community normalcy to raise radical reason
We have been duped by fanning sharks of the South Sea reefs who mesmerize us with their whirling fans of dubious
death Arise now and find the four truth shields and block all tremulous and continual attacks upon our perilous four

Seeking New Possibilities

Envision how I will refill
There is a gap to be closed
Rethink how to cement it
Gaps are caused by faults
Wherein lies fault causes
I will investigate cracks
I become expert on cracks
My hat:Break commission
A commissioner of cracks
Find the root fissure cause
My life role will be finding constant breaks as route repairman
My fulfillment is to fill gapping gaps and make me whole again
seek new possibilities but only I can fill the knowledge gaps
seek new possibilities but only I can fix a gapping gap ahead
Gaps are the roadblocks given in life to aggressively overcome

Helping to Find keys to Life's Satisfaction

We constantly seek the next thrill over the hill to be complete
Here it is only an empty valley called the Ridge of Lost Souls
Can we speak freely and understand who is behind our hope
Have we been so barraged that we are accepting tank tempters
Tank tempters fill our brains with arcane thoughts and ideas
Are we so lost in thick woodlands that we cannot think straight
Seek Clarity pathways and Sound Trail markers Be enlightened
When we fail to think for ourselves we hide in deep foglands
Our mission is to constantly test opinions and forays of others
Otherwise we may become owners of 5,000 acres of quicksand
Stand your own thoughts into elastic bags and sort them all out
Tomorrow and the day after you will be pressed to think wisely
Arise as The Great Paragon of Wisdom and test all these things
You were given a brain to arrive at a Station of Clear Thinking
Reorganize and march to the clear music of persistent revival

Catalina Island

A ferry leads across the expanse of water to my Catalina
Forging across the massive bay I see schools of dolphins
Somehow they have confused us with chasing predators
The ebb and flow of the moving sea water is exuberant
Finally the dolphins now realize it is only people to fear
I continue across a bustling archipelago then observe land
From an edge of my ferry I now see Mount Orizaba rise
Then I come in closer and see an azul bay cove at Avalon
There is something special about a Channel Island chain
These islands represent old California before a remake
I am mesmerized by times preservation of a few strands
Native people are gone and native plants decimated here
Yet on the margins of liquid time Islands remains intact
Catalina wallows in the curvature of a delayed progress
I will enjoy all echoes of yesterday until a grand remodel

Two Irises in February

I watch the Arizona sun trifle with the stem rise of two Irises
The nights will play cool breezes on my tiny front courtyard
Yet unfolding and unwrapping of the white lavender is magic
I envision this uplifting stalk of mid winter as a glowing signal

Now I will raise a garden
Now I will refeed lawns
Now I will prune decay
Now I will cut end branch
Now I will realign all rows
Today is the new day rise
Now I will transplant all
Eminent days have come
Signs of rebirth will show
I see Irises change the day

27

Probing Our Great Wonderment

We are people created to create and then recreate our lives on a continual pattern of wonderment
Time flows on the rivers of life quickly and we are at creations wheel observing all that we appreciate
Then as we come closer to the end stream we enjoy recreating all that was pleasant in our pathway
Our definition of wonderment will slightly differ from our surrounding compatriots due to our pathos
Each individual created has a unique pathos that drives their soul to reach a specific full life conclusion
Awareness of the trail to follow becomes a sojourn through life... a passage to a personal wonderment

Amassing Our Mindset at the Railroad Station

With little time to meditate I hear the train whistle blow its warning toot
My time is limited so thoughts of the day begin to slow flow and drift
How I must plan the tasks or activities to completion or a stopping point
I must do a sterling job for my silver nosed boss now on the up structure
All finite details must be lock tight to allow the answers to free fall once
I must be the springboard for the success of the masses that may grapple
Great story lines will be the verbiage to get through the mass monotony
Keep the work flow racing toward the final terminal with great velocity
Commit to all real work possibilities and keep questions from snagging
I am the trumpeter of everyones success ...depend on me for completion
I am a to do locomotive puffing as a nightmare keeping bodies moving

Saving Sanity Forever

Often we are shocked by radical behavior since it is beyond our real norm
Shaking we try to explain obtuse actions of others when they occur in time
Primarily we focus on the causes and the effects of all the negative behavior
Yet answers lie in the soul of individuals as they act on Irresponsible Avenue
Mind demonstrations are part of the psyche of each explosion that happens
When the soul allows the flood of justification to enter then a battle begins
Timing becomes the only issue in the heart when the final explosion erupts
Racing down a morass of madness demons gather to assist all maniac culprits
Slaughter of the innocents occur so no witnesses survive the mad onslaught
While we cannot identify all the corridors of mindless craziness that amass
We can only identify smoldering pots and do everything to put the fires out
Sanity can only be revived forever through corridors of understanding love

Fort Royal Nova Scotia

Reconstructed it somehow stands now a row of renown wood amassed
Protecting an inlet bay and coastline a bastion of English resistance
Often repelling attacks from independent sources it stood the testing well
Redcoats ruled the inner sanctum of the beehive bastion of resistance
This small wooden fort repelled any charging invaders with cannons
Sitting on the precipice of a hill it was an undaunting aged edifice here
Serving as a reminder for those who challenge its raw power and might
Casting a shadow on a land itself keeping Nova Scotia under the crown
Loyal and royal it remains a significant trace of a bygone era of strife

28

His Magnum Opus

Working diligently he created much
Yet we knew there was more to come
One October morning we heard a cry
Cries of joy-elation-accomplishment
His great painting *Alluring Conquest*
This work was his grand masterpiece
The artist completed it in twenty days
A timeless work of ardent Surrealism
We saw a dreamlike image occurring
Angry charging irridescent dragons
All appearing with wide open jaws
Massive teeth with shining imagery
In a center all three dragons tongues
Battles now waged on lashed tongues
Three dragons three tongues one war
A war of hopeless hemorrhaging hell
We were phased by this iconic image
Has our human race reached madness
Did a artist canvas dream endless hell
Did an artist paint flow his thoughts
A reigning sordid uncivilized image
Tomorrow this vivid image will sell
Reality has amassed a stinging price

Canto to a Continuum

I will move forward and sing a song
My life had different roles and reals
The real part did not always play out
The real part oozed in some places
Yet I kept playing long positive notes

Several times my roles changed fast
I adapted quickly to the new music
Continually I sang to requested music
Culture changed I adapted humming
Yet I kept playing long positive notes

People that peopled over my work
They worked to mass reverberation
My part a one note piece of a puzzle
Sometimes the music was invisible
Yet I kept playing long positive notes

Many times when the music was fast
I traced a diagram for expected notes
When all failed to show up I whistled
My whistling caught their attention
I continued to play long drawn notes

When they failed to read my notes
When they did not understand music
Then played Smoke gets in your eyes
Thought I mesmerized but I slipped
Then was memorialized in long notes

Time's One Moment of Evolved Creation

At the appointed time.... right now
Blaring excitement permeates here
Created forces have intertwined all
There is planned formation of life
Newness prevails with aliveness
Massive mercurial motion made
Look upon the cataclysmic voice
CREATION begins with a bang
A roaring grand swirl commences
Aligning with wisdom reaching
Multiple Universes begin cresting
Moving inter galactic forces pull
A vast array of planetary placings
Then a hurling stone hemorrhage
Followed by a pentagon separation
Multiple universe define pathways
A settling drifting calm prevails
One moment of creation is defined

Braving the Storm

Horrific winds scrape the landscape
Rounding our house we see power
It is our mindset to pray and hope
When we emerge from tiny shelters
What will our mass reaction be then

How will we cope with what remains
Perhaps all is well as we rise upward
Opening our bulkhead we see it all
Only Aunt Minerva's old outhouse
Yes that is all the tornado took out

A toilet seat hangs from a lone pine
This is our reminder of destruction
Animals are exceptionally nervous
Slowly we go and calm them down
Without power we key our kerosene

All three lamps are lit and we sleep
Guardedly we will sleep on haylofts
Our animals make confident sounds
We are powerless predicting twisters
yet we are powerful with our actions

Twisters do monumental destruction
We need to assure our own trail ways

Sightings in a Distance

Numerous times I ran for clear cover
I saw the growing madness occurring
Those who were ossified were angry
You may be chosen for their great ire
Your face could become a sure target
I see my head is not a punching bag
Avoiding the gorilla growl is my call
Initially when a roaring drunk roars
Then I see a door as an escape route
Waiting can accrue loose teeth blood
Mocous madness makes for mayhem
Allow your senses quick processing
Sighting from a distance is real sanity
Allow the boys in blue great latitude
They will carry swinging parts to rest
Allow the gorillas to wail in their jail
Tomorrow a significant buzz occurs
Buzz number one is a huge headache
Buzz number two is drunk disorderly
Buzz number three pay paddy wagon
Buzz number four is a misdemeanor
Buzz number five is a broken jaw
Buzz number six you lost your job
It was a brilliant beerbuzzed weekend
Later he jumps a Mystic River Bridge
This was an unexpected distant sight

New Energies Propelling Me

While I am a who I am I see new life
Masses of energy fuels my re-psyche
It must drive me to a new Euphoria
I will ask the train conductor where
Please announce a new Euphoria stop
I must disembark here : be recharged
Where can I drive a new Re-purpose
Where can I create a real New image
Where can the drum beat of life Redo
Where can I re-assemble my Ideals
I will find a powerful sense of ecstasy
I will arrive at feelings of new elation
I will inspire to a new set of rituals
I will transpire to a new at now vision

Finding new energy can be a search
moving out of the old cocoon is work
Unwrapping of layers takes time now
Yet deep inside I hear a call to revise
Aligning my day and reconfigure all
It is never too late to change the You
I remember Anne Sawitsky said so
Therefore a Grand engine is moving
Recycle your everything : It begins!!

Resting on our Accomplishments

There are instances where we accept accolades for a great performance often done by others

When the call is made we are waiting in the anteroom to accept someone else's achievement

How is it possible that this occurs and creative energies are given shabby last row treatment

Perhaps this might be a test for how wayward brilliance must practice massive self-restraint

My chain reaction rumbles when others bask in a glory since they were totally disconnected

Perhaps it could happen to me as I rant and rave about my own greatness with no credentials

Somehow on the horizon of times alarm clock we will get a chance to allow others to bask

Focus on how others will take their cue to accept credit for our great and gratuitous works

Bite your tongue remain amused when you stopped playing golf with boss a worm did turn

Resting on prior accomplishments tends to raise the flag that you are presently idea empty

Zig Zag

When I am faced with difficult decisions I motion my brain

Often lifting the cover my brain cells are in denial of any crisis

My inner thoughts turn to mush and I cave into extreme avoidance

Fear or indecision can cause tidal waves by my frozen sense to act

At other times I run quick gridiron patterns untouched and so safely

Friends comment on my adroitness as real points of great praise

Becoming a hero does little to wash my non response in life

Deliberate must be a new invective: life must be dealt with terms

The pattern my mother used sewing my pants and shirts had a merit

The weave was strong solid and true withstanding a times testing

Reforming a new image I need to have gumption and guts to change

Tomorrow I will argue my overcharge on the electric bill I have

I will perform a Zig Zag motion that dazzles the Electric man

30

Riding the Rave

Great people remain sane galloping
Carefully they quickly ride a Rave
When the Rave ends they resettle
Finding a different steed they slow
Changing speeds gives a real boost
By controlling their personal gait
Cross the finish line remembered

Contemplating

Musing is an easy past time for me
Several times I saw positive ends
Visualize possibilities for direction
Others may not agree with me so
take my deep thoughts seriously
Far better having a real focus here
Use my talent to move new ideas
My vociferous to renewable ideas
These ideas may not ring to you
Yet I am thinking and musing now
What am I contemplating to now?
Be gratefully surprised : My focus
Change the Rigid avenues soon
Smooth the Angry worn gutters
Repave the Warped lined streets
Replant the Stately boulevards
Revamp all sidewalks smoothly
Repair the Chipped curbstones
If a king comes am I in readiness?

Hope Can Save Us

Trying to do our finite best dwells
Our mind will stand for perfection
Not accepting less than greatness
Rounding out effort is a thought
Brain cells need to be commandeered
Allegiances must be sought after
Finding the true believers difficult
Oneness in meaning and majesty
Planning our strategy to success
Success translates to one purpose
Rise at the early horizon of day
Seek the open door of engagement
Walk through the opening and see
Your life is written on a gray tablet
Have you met your grand objective?
Often we need to replan and restep
Basic instruction before leaving earth
Scroll.. agree... and mark your place!

Joy is Contagious

Joy is wrapped in my personal me
I can share the moment with you
I can exude a flow overwhelming
I observe the pouring over and out
I see it raging as a high floodplain
I welcome its true cleansing power
Joy is the pouring out..all excesses
Joy is the pouring in..all perfection
Joy lead me to a ever flowing river
Drink from the streams of joy now
Channel my life to an observation
I see those in joy settling in peace

Help is Arriving

Plans are constructed on a chalkboard
Time erases initial unpractible plans
Wisdom arrives as a helpful aide now
Reconstructing we locate small errors
We discover original plans as defunct
Revised plans need restructure often

Grand wizen of revision has decision
Architects will redirect a new dialect
Calls come out of the walls of halls
Do not renege but repeg all four legs
Resettle tiers to provide sheer to piers
Finalize the eyes of certain blue skies
Share a lamp to revamp a new camp
Arise to the surprise of formalize
Then we are redone as a pun in a sun

Finding the Final Outcome

Houses shake and creak in the Gale storm
Often lights dim or go out indefinitely
Struggling everyone up the coast effected
Alarms go out to low lying areas : floods
The coastline just at sea level collapses
Rudimentary dykes fall -sea walls cave in
Man is no match for the raging sea storm
The sea water eats up the landscape fast
A howling mass of riveting rain drives us
We become nervous hens in the henhouse
The driving twisting storm continues mad
Can we change a disposition of the Gale?
Can we somehow outfox the nasty storm?
Can we relegate the excess rain to a hole?
Can we collect electric drops to convert?
Can we bring mass chaos to subduction?
Can we find a pattern of climate control?
Ingenuity is a projected patterned resolve

This our Group Conscious

Wrestle about seven precarious problems
All decisions are made by a valiant cadre
Idealism can prevail yet practicality also
Since we are but a few be clear minded
All catapulting group decisions are heavy
Somehow wisdom must prevail as intact
Finding answers : A new massive search
Ending our group seance we are to action
Search delivers a huge impact as a plan
Issue 1 Rotate angry members on skewer
Issue 2 Raise Screaming People to a door
Issue 3 Find a solution to non-problems
Issue 4 Locate seats for ungrateful brats
Issue 5 Prime sink holes for complainers
Issue 6 Help the brain washed to rebrain
Issue 7 Seek bridges for those marooned

Our arduous tasks are mounting quickly
Our call to action is always immediate
We are a group of conscientious cattails
We are never satisfied until tails uncurl
Those we help are often beyond our help
Offering a rope to recharge is group guts
We never leave meetings without clarity
Those in need are always given choices
March in a morning toward final answers
We provide what others fail to provide
Between dial a prayer and blub blub blub

Transvector

Different challenges invade us in our trek
Often we are redirected onto new angles
Then we redirect our approach to life
New angles redirect pathways and trails
Our thought patterns are changed rapidly
We send out octopus ink to confuse some
Our perceived enemies become confused
Taking a new plan to follow we succeed
Multitudes of madmen become real angry
Our mission creates a smooth flow now
Our fundamental challenge belongs still
Issues fade into a fog mist for others now
Rise over the transvectored mad masses
We have become the outliers of success

Rolling Through the thicket

Where I walk there is no trail to follow
My resort is to push through the thicket
Once the bushes and tall grass is crushed
New trails can begin to lead forward now
New destinations will be located sooner
Crisscross patterns may create efficiency
New trails can provide for simple passage
I am instructed to always plan Improvise
Improvise is a trail leading to New Vista
New Vista :A next rising Majestic Project

Enjoying Our Amusements

Little tea cups did a swirl
Little children did a curl
Rotate revolve so to unfurl
Moves make us feel a hurl
Lock us in a necklace burl

Then all will laugh : time passed when we did scream
Find time to laugh: our memories told it was a dream
Yet we understand amusements always made us beam
Amusements were the machines that got us to gleam

Round and round motion made us lose our ice Cream
We close our eyes and then we see a bubbling stream
This all we had seen amidst a puff of fantastic steam

Our amusements are what keep us excited and racing
Then our jittering nervous souls will keep us pacing
No time to slow down to perceive what we are facing
A crisis is arising so we are hot wired without bracing
Events kept us busy we failed to double tie our lacing
Yet windows of wonderment have not been a tracing
Emotional traps so growing we are finding no spacing
Our lives are so fast paced we wrap without a basing
Catastrophe hits us with no time to allow for erasing

Just as Friends

In Vermont we caught up to the old times
Refreshed our memories and did a fill in
Time has passed so in seven years change
Change and rearrange in lives we know
Tomorrow even more revising will occur
While we are powerless to revise all lives
Together we can talk on future life plans
Yet today we are together just as friends

As we tethered our conversation we knew
Stories criss cross to be part of lifes flow
Often there is uplift sometime down shift
Our mortality gleams so we are part hope
We link to others even when so unaware
Great words are passed on as time erases
We build relationships on a solid ground
Time will erode but foundation is strong

We can smile even know ups and downs
The river of life passes ferociously here
Our only control is our real compassion
Reaching out soon we become a signpost
Then we evolve becoming a true anchor
When our families are adrift we are help
When those around need assistance : Yes
Our life evolves becoming listening ears

The Great Steamer

The old steamer was a classic in her time
Breaking through Lake Champlain waters
Even on stormy nights she was a beauty
Able to withstand rain and strong winds
She hovers with a grace of a white swan
Her moves were so defined and graceful
Coming and leaving port was a rhapsody
All were timed with the clarity of a crew
Crew members were totally hand picked
Then our captain knew everyones foibles
knowing their weakness he matched men
Alert keeping guard for safety and sanity
Through all charted water calm prevails
She is a delivery gem on Lake Champlain
Powerful wheel paddle navigates perfect
Driving all lake waters to usual balances
She sits in port as moving compartments
When needs are great sleep berths ready
When a need is wanting sick bay is ready
When a current is strong steering ready
When the snows fly her visability is acute
When vital personages arrive she is clean
Mirroring she glides across as waterbug
For multitude destinations she is flexible
For ports of call shes always in readiness

For her final voyage her flags flew proud

Cape May Beaches Abound

Arriving on the beach and relaxing here
Cape May is our stretch and fresh breath
All the Gingerbread trellis is our charm
We enjoy our pleasant surroundings now
Time on the beach front is enchantment
We hover around yesterdays amusement
Machines Date their origin yet we enjoy
Finding a favorite cupola or widow walk
This adds to our momentary readventure
Time has passed yet we revel in the past
Color our lives with quieter time or place
We revere in journeys to olde Cape May

In the great summer season waves crash
In the distance sail boats angle in a wind
In the summer New Jersey shore uplifts
In the wide white dunes we build a castle
In the afternoon the tide recedes to flats
In the tidepools many small sea creatures
In the brief adventure we collect seashells
In the water small minnows dart all about
In the wave action pieces of Sea kelp bob
In the hot sunshine beach umbrellas is an
In the swimming lessons we learn how to
In the days end we wipe off all the sand

Cape Cod Bay

Sand becomes our pathway to the bay. It eases our walk and slows us down...Then we can appreciate the quiet beach

Muscle of Massachusetts

Quickly it flexes its wide arm and allows you to observe a symetrical array of natures creation ordered as inlets dunes and sandcoves
Rolling across a winding landscape it bridges out into the Atlantic to give you the feel of the Gulf Stream Current wending away East
While I observe the great miniclimate wild life abounds amongst humanity since there is allocated open space for all to once coexist
Across the crystal sand and marshes the habitant remains a prestigious monument allowing flora and fauna to flourish in abundance
When gray Atlantic produces a fury the muscle closes all the natural doors and prepares for an inundated rain flow with turbulence
n aftermath of a washdown masses of brilliant flowers array their approval waving their push petals in a unreliquished mass approval

Twin trees bridging

Twin trees dance now
They hold branches
Their dance is round
A circle cycle dance
Around and around
It appears so moving
They stand so proud as the Lone Monterrey Cypress
Yet their demonstrative dance is hard to compare to
observe their movement as a wonderful act of art
Majestic arms are raised in triumph to show a style
see a Jose Greco Flamenco dance clicking to music
am wowed by the open space and calm background
Tomorrow the sun will penetrate and repeat this act

Arriving at the great Terminal Bristling

Tomorrow is the discovery day in my life as I leave for adventure
Planning was the action of my life that I have not as yet learned
A great massive jet will take me airborne to new exciting destinations
must prepare myself for great challenges allowing for expectations
have been gifted with a great mind and have been selected to use it
My journey begins today I am bound for Ivy league and know to soak
will seek the best and inhale great knowledge to prepare for futures
Delivery is my keynote and no matter how difficult the course matter
will chart an agressive course and observe the forward pathways
My trail is now being opened and I will stay a course of my ancestors
When I arrive I will open my friendships and become a great sponge

Climbing the Himalayas

High peaks and challenges lay before me as I begin my great ascent
Yet my life has always been a massive challenge and upward climb
There is a change of altitude that I must prepare for with oxygen ready
There is a change of attitude that I must adjust for and think of others
There is a change of latitude I must focus on the heights and a mindset
There is a change of gratitude that I must allow for those who assisted

Himalayas are more than words in a travel magazine they are aspiring
Himalayas are gargantuan mountain peaks rising upward and inspiring
Himalayas are in my mindset and have totally gripped me as admiring
Himalayas are on my approval list to have passed a test of my desiring
Himalayas are rising on my to do list as a testimony of my prioritizing
Himalayas are a high challenge I may never meet so I am phantisizing

Bubbles can forget my Troubles

Often the simple life
Often simple actions
A few Bubbles do rise
I see the issue vacate
Troubles capture me
I need to see them go
So Bubbles rise away
Once a wind takes them into the heights I can smile
Every Bubble is a designated trouble to be released
Every Bubble is lifted up and off my shoulders now
Every Bubble represents an anguish and a madness
Going forward a pent up problem is erased forever

33

The Forest is A Great Enchantment

Walking through the ancient eastern forest I see the marks of civilization as I rapidly move across this grand landscape
Around the bends in well worn trails are granite boulders soon delivered by an ice age past so I sometimes stop and sit
Yet this fabulous woodland yields a grand abundance of ancient trees that cover the landscape with magnificent shades
Yes it is multiple colors of their spreading branches that allows me to escape my reality as I walk in great enchantment
It is these quiet trail walks that give me a spark of significant creativity that permeate ideas in my genesis brain caverns
A great unfolding occurs as the interconnect of thunderous thoughts constantly collide with an amassed clashing logic
Profound thoughts can grow into magnificent ideas and agendas that may revise one mans thought or the entire world

Rhode Island Roads

I travelled down Seapowet and there was a light fog dancing on the road
My road trail took me into a deep hollow and then into a sharp left turn
Seapowet dances in the mist and I am amazed that everything stands still
Soon after nine o'clock a fog lifts and a well travelled road appears now
Lush green flowers and grass line a roadside and my eyes are given rest
Clarity on the Rhode Island Road keeps me breathing freely so peaceful
Continuing down to Sakonnet River I see a beach at Fogland and rejoice
My green pastures and still waters actual exist at one place in time space
Going forward I resolve to revisit this place so my eyes are not deceived
Tomorrow I do follow this road again so I reassure my souls one vision

Grand Entrance

There is always a grand entre way into the homes of family and friends
Often we cherish such a rockery welcome with a high rising rose trellis
Then we see the arching oaks saluting sassafras and at attention poplars
This could be a great welcoming for a princely entourage charging ahead
Perhaps this may serve as a riveted pathway to announce a new wedding
Then again this could be one setting for a major political announcement
Maybe we could launch a major cocktail party for a surprise new merger
This could be a beginning of a great narrative novel not quite finished
Thinking ahead it may be a gilded road ahead set for our final departure
Yet real time announced..... Aahi Tuna supper will be held at five o'clock

Round Barns

Round barns are a cycle reminded me that farmers chores are never done
It is in the mystical round I sense that all agrarian work runs in a round
Yet on each level of the round unique work is accomplished tediously
Profound dedication and love of this life style creates a patient mindset
Crops do not grow without downpours so I will wait very quiet and calm
Cows do not deliver their dairy expectation unless coddled and fed well
Pigs will not produce the bacon we are aching for without loads of slop
Sheep fail to render their wool unless given the will to meander all over
Fences barns and silos do not hold up storage and shelter unless attended
Rectangle barns do say 'Chew Mail Pouch Tobacco' Round Barns do no

Coming to Our Crossroads - Forever Focused Resilent

Decision time was often an obtuse period in my life when I was groping for significant right answers walking a very cautious pathway
How can I predict all the correct trails when I really do not know all the specific end destinations in my lifes real perpetual journey
After several walks and trail tracings I have tested some outcomes that will not work so I continue to trace what lies ahead for now
Often others who have been hikers on the trail can tell you of the massive greatness and the acute shortcomings yet you must walk
As I pace myself ahead quickly eventually I arrive at a fork in a road and my decision map must then lead me to take accurate moves
Now I am at a grand life crossroad I observe that I must peal through the great credenza of my mind and make a lifetime decision
Since I am constructed in the tenets of logic and my heritage bleeds of these logic building blocks I will chose challenge trail at LEFT
Yes to my LEFT there are many high points to climb a few mass objects to avoid and several detours yet I am forever focused resilent

Reaching for the Sky

On the vast redwood forest floor I am amazed at all pointing skyward
Perhaps I see every living thing desiring the access to the open sunlight
Then again.... is it a symbol of great praise to be part of a redwood flora
Magnificent dripping dew and grand aromas surround a grand red carpet
This redwood floor can breathe a special breath of continual resurrection
Out of the sides of massive fallen redwoods new trees align and depart
Something in a redwood culture continues to magnify this new growth
Trees are reborn to create a cycle of persisitence and determination here
I wave to all the ferns and forest flowers that herald gradiose redwoods
Tomorrow I will be reaching for the sky encircled by redwood masses

Royal Hibiscus

Luna Pink Swirl is my Merl who resembles a pearl who likes to swirl
Often I see a wind make them furl into a real magnificent double curl
They like to twirl as a ferris wheel enjoying its favor making it whirl
After I spoke with a girl who showed me noise came from a bush burl
Yet my friend Earl was awhirl upon seeing the center of hibiscus knurl
So I told my bargirl friend Patty Unchurl to investigate to give it a shirl
Then as the wind slowed down I made it unfurl into a knit 1 then 2 perl
So then these hibiscus began to hurl onto each other like a mass of churl
What winds accomplished aswirl looks different than a dashing squirrel
Now Luna pink swirl is in a massive whorl flapping in our windy world

Departure Depot

Commuters patiently await an express train to our specified destination
All are anticipating a smooth ride to an end of the line where plans await
Friends and family bid us travellers safe journey to Nine Patient Prairie
I know we all are going to places of reknown a real unforgetable trip
Initially I saw tumbleweed rolling to then later vermillion hills to climb
After awhile cattle grazed and moved as a herd after two coyotes howled
A lamp seen at a distance around campfires where cowboys sang ballads
Tomorrow I pass through red rock canyon designated a haven of serenity
Not long after I come to Sweetwater River that cascades to Patient Lake
Instantly I see no return trip since I see my soul gazed through my life

Calling us to the Rises

A clarion call we hear is to be real involved
Then we become occupied with a two mission
Our two mission becomes one of great service
We rise and see the needs and address them
Yes one by one we must now stretch ourselves
Once we are called to the rises action sends us
We must assume a activity playbook to move
So go to the altar of acceptance and accept it
Our two mission delivers this joy and peace
As we deliver these elements serenity comes
Once we have accomplished the two mission
Then we will rise to the next level for words
A word is Go forth: Behold a new beginning

Primary

Primary is the school that I was told to attend
then when I arrived they taught primary colors
As I learn colors they painted brilliant ideas
Mass of ideas were awash as penmanship won
Boldly I formed words as ideas blossomed
First there was.. gnoop then parselick to zei
Of course then massa de gerp as for lepprasst
Teachers discovered my talent in pen scrolls
We never know how talent arises so quickly
Mass amounts of researchers are analyzing
Research said Lepprasst is a town at Niniveh
Then of course Gnoop is a old Sumerian word
At last Massa de gerp was a Phoenician ship
I found that Parselick to zei is a river in Persia
Tomorrow I pen my stream of consciousness
I allow my scrolls to recreate a hidden word
My primary purpose is plugged into circles
My life evolves to a continual cycle of circles
So when will your primary purpose emerge

Drum Roll

A drum roll is delivered for those who passed
In the stillness of evening his spirit passed on
He was a strong minded Captain who fought
He covered a lot of territory as zone protector
When a fire fight began he covered his troops
Being last one to leave the zone he retraced all
This is when he took a shot through the heart
His men fought back and retrieved his body
Our enemy deserves no bodily remains here
They returned to camp with a Captains body
A single drum roll declared his new departure
He has been reassigned to heaven a new zone

Auntie Pastow

I learned I had a special aunt I never knew
She came to me as a unique treat one evening
I was expecting a real wonderful loud noise
Yet Auntie Pastow was real quiet unassuming
She sat down next to me and promptly rose
Her special aroma was quite unique and real
After I put my fork into her I found delight
However later I had Aunt Gerd all the night
My stomach lost a battle taste buds won a war

BURNED SIENNA

When I carefully colored pictures in a book
All lines were full but never breached here
My cousin remarked what I should have used
Use burned sienna on the roof of the shed
This is the correct color to use on that roof
I saw and used gray since nothing was on fire
My cousin was fired up due to a wrong color
I tore out the page and burned sienna flamed

Rising to meet my Transformation

Yesterday I was informed I should make a list
Slowly I constructed a loose list of my habits
All the imperfections I was willing to admit
Finding this scarecrow list uneventful I seek
Of course a list is only an outline of search
Real deep search is a tumultous task for me

I seek to get under my buttons and push them
I seek to observe what others have-do I need it
I heard my loud voice bellow I tone it down
I sense disagreements become arguments-why
I seek to rid myself of wild brash decisions
I seek to see others in their best possible light

All my imperfections add to growing tell lists
All my marginally developed attributes show
All my transcendent ideas about me are shaky
All my behaviors illustrate my shortcomings
All my attitudes show my approach to my life
All the opinions of others are often unfounded

Therefore I will be thorough to totally honest
Therefore I will seek change A great rearrange
Therefore I will tone down all the me buttons
Therefore I must make solid recommitments
Therefore I will try to make sound decisions
Thus doing my key modifications I transform

As I rise I see my contorted self as an image
As I rise I observe how others react to change
As I rise I am making a commitment to rebirth
As I rise I see the need for additional changes
As I rise there are those who judge my redo
As I rise I do realize one tranformation leads..

Centering

Nuetralize my existence so my words collapse
Profound actions effect a totality of prescence
Either I will listen carefully or remain so mute
Structures of lifes laybrinth need my attention

When there is a need to compromise I must be
I must be a truce giver moving toward center
Declaring a cease fire parties need rediscovery
Centering is round tables a face to face action

Obstancy can be a position for stale mate now
Revelation can be an attitude of massive move
Moving out of a high fog layer observe now
Centering unveils a dual awareness of change

Possibilities

See my lifes journey is full of real possibilities
Climbing out of back seat I am now in control
I will drive my life forward with new passion
There is no slowdown since life is galloping
Delve into the radical changes occuring now
I am ready to barge out of new rooms quickly
Culture change is rapidly rocking the society
There are no existing norms to capture now
So I must weigh all possibilities upon ruling
My fate is locked in a cell of glad assurances
I cannot predict a future in a real flux culture
Tomorrow my possibilities range at I thru 10
Every move through a maze of life examined
I will cluster my thoughts on a triumph board
I will declare a possible fulfillment in AMEN

Mentoring

While I assist others there is massive conflict
My mission must be to spend time and assist
I need to allocate blocks of time for transition
Knowledge needs to build and feed my brains
Once fed then I may distribute this word food
Carefully I need to separate opinion from fact
My mentoring should lead others to a reflect
Learning by spoon fed mentoring is so intense
Sometimes I need to step aside to an observer
Observers can restructure a message different
Mentors need to deliver mentoring in variety
A variety shows those being mentored ways
Ways are several mentored processes to work
Discover the Mentor magic that opens a heart
When the heart agrees the mentor is complete

Entering Serenity Lake

I rose into an empty canoe left for my journey
When my life was out of control this was here
Here are two paddles to drive me across now
Needing no push I paddle onto Serenity Lake
I fought my demons and they won the battle
Now I need to regroup my thoughts into peace
I am bruised only temporarily so I bandage up
All scars are recoverable so I row with fervor
In the distance is the house I elected to stay at
I am greeeted at a door of Rediscovery House
Tomorrow I will read the Serenity code of life
Tomorrow I commence rediscovering myself
Tomorrow I will let the spirit of chaos leave
Tomorrow I will meditate on A Serenity lake
Tomorrow the God of my understanding sees
Tomorrow a full veil is lifted from my vision
Tomorrow the agents of reconstruction work
All agents will sponsor my complete renewal
My amplified anxiety and anger still remains
My sinful self centered self is still singed now
My broken bottle of beer bent in my thoughts
All agents remind me time heals a brokeness
All agents bring me to the restoration rooms
All agent meditate for my binding wholeness
In these rooms I hear real massive brokeness
In these room people roll cringe and sob soft
In these rooms I heard all so serenity binds m

Avalanche

Masses of snow lay heavy on these hills
Danger lurks in the overweighted breaks
As the slow treacherous melt commences
Daily worry marks the faces of the rescue
If there is strong wind a fast melt...cracks
When breaks shake then there is a slipper
Slippers unanchor from the heights down
A roar of snow powder fills the surround
Then mass breakage send tons downward
Those below are at the mercy of the path
Paths of avalanches are unpredicable here
Yes Today we dig out ourselves so alone
Tomorrow we count to see all casualties
Tomorrow we find out if we are a number

Palliotis

When I hear the prognosis labeled now
When words have settled in the rooms
A stalwart and seasoned physician says
Well you have palliotis primeria boccus
While I am unsure of the end result of it
Here I lay in a pensive predicament now
The physician hails the contagious nurse
She wears a red bandana for protection
She carefully sprays a lemon balm elixer
This elixer eradicates the Palliotis germs
Now I begin to smell like a lemon danish
I am then reassured by the medical staff
Spray balm in your mouth for one month
Return to us, if all is well you will be free
I am unsure what captures us and frees us
I do know that I will be balmy one month
After this I will return to a state of sanity
Lemon elixer must beat out orange twist

Tomato Jubilee

There is something about a first one of season
It may be a refreshing tarty acidy flavor taste
Perhaps that first juicy gush that satisfies now
Then as a tender slice it gives other food a zip
No other vegatable that is regal fruit compares
Beyond words the real unique taste is a rarity
Let us rise and create a jeweled tomato jubilee
Tomorrow we celebrate a beefsteak or cherry

Capturing the Now Moment

Our heart flutters as we remember death
People leave us in real random formation
How some of us survive remains a puzzle
We were given a purpose to be uncovered
An ardent search is part of personal DNA
Structures surround us for us to discover

Discovery is part of our inquisitive nature
Our plan unfolds in front of our own eyes
Once we remove a blockage light arrives
We begin to comprehend a guided trail
We must light the luminarias to be aware
Messages hang as guideposts to follow

Our perception commences as we do see
A plan in the road instucts us to Where
Where is a map that yields true answers
Our mission is to translate configurations
We capture the now moment on a trail
Analyze the data and move to an Action

Open yourself to a kaleidiscope of life
Delaying our reality is a nonaction now
You were given a specific mission bell
Ring the bell and trace the configuration
Time has come to move forward indeed
Your now moment must be acted upon!

My Fate in Babylon

Sitting in the Hanging Gardens of Babylon
My vision has been clouded by oleanders
Masses of green ivy dangle from the walls
Boughs of lilacs arch over slate pathways
This is a place in my dreams come alive

Perhaps I am a dreamer at unothodox times
I percieve I am at these gardens for a reason
Musing at one of the seven ancient wonders
Now I ponder an Emperor Nebuchednezzar
Why were these gardens ever constructed

At the beckoning of Queen Amytis a rise
A great massive rise and a flower fortress
Oh yes and Babylon is the Gate of the Gods
Enter now with tree lined shade tree cover
Enter now with gardens tier upon tier rising

I sit by the Euphrates observing a water flow
I sit and perceive the huge irrigated canals
These canals rise to aqeducts pouring forth
The flow of water gushes through gardens
Sluice gates open to aromatic flower beds

I am now in a trance sitting near a river bank
Palm trees rise upon tops of massive pillars
This quadrangular garden risen by four arches
A marvelous structure elevating to my zenith
A most joyous uplifting and pleasing edifice

Was it a phenominal finger of fate driving me
Yes I must be stuck in a dated time warp now
First I was in the garden and then at a distance
My focus was both internal and external here
Hanging Gardens of Babylon was my mirage

I will locate mirages occuring in my life span
For the many fields of flowers I see memories
For the multi tiered edifices I see great hope
For the rushing waterfalls I observe the power
For continuous waves I feel a great cleansing

Profound Collaboration

Earth relies on the collaboration of many men
Often man becomes innovative and reckless
Yet earth needs a gentle touch and adolation
Often mankind is rough and collectively crude
Earth may desire a complete origin restoration
Expansive nature of man revises sky and mud
Earth pleads to have its crust cared for gently
Obtuse nature of man melt ice cap and drowns

Complex Interlude

Magnificent meetings lead to exciting endings
Facinating accomplishments are challenges
Discovering pathways leads to breakthrough
Our universe moves at a phenominal speed
Obsessed with remarkable accuracy we smile
Travelling at unrestricted speeds we explore
Then a huge complex interlude forms a shift
Words fail to describe two galaxies colliding

Created Clusters Aligning

Motion in a universe of Luminicence complex
Laws of man define to design to explain space
Space is an ever expanding illusion of forces
Mans laws do not apply into deep space warp
Acceleration of galaxies cross paths in voids
Sudden space phenomena is discovered seen
Countless collisions by a gravitational force
Some obtuse action delivers long energy burst
Mind boggling concepts redo scientific papers
Restoration in multiple changes can be frothy
Some scholars fume when their idea is a melt
Space Travellers must be calm and conscience
Leadership and followship is masked by intent
On extraordinary alignment we are astounded
Great crested clusters do remain intact forever

Planning the Ideal Meal

I listen to chef masters who give a great spiel
Kitchen Commanders who plan a special meal
Yet my focus is too slow to adjust to their feel
Squeeze pinch takes too much time for appeal
I fail to reshuffle my time slot to do this deal
I need to gather my strength with greater zeal
I listened one day and jotted instructions real
Tomorrow I will deliver Ponte de Verde Veal

The Great Granite Quarries

I remember my father reminicing of quarries
Migrations of Swedes Finns and Italians came
Yes they were the ones that knew quarry work
How to carefuly remove great granite chunks
They were agile dedicated and knowledgeable
With great precision the teamwork had results
Massive stones are moved hydraulically now
Yes granite is honed shaped and polished well
Granite is moved down stream on raftbarges
Finished stone is delivered to the build sites
Much of Bostons old city is built on granite
Yes Quincy granite built old Boston skyward

Comprehensive

Is it my desire to cover everything completely
Let no stone remain unless its overturned here
My coverage of life will touch all facets I see
I will write down all details and give a speech
I can make it plain so all clearly understand it
As people grasp the tiers of my detail massage
Tomorrow I will commence adding a structure
My intent is to be fully finite so comprehesive

Mercy

One of my most difficult concepts is of mercy
This would be shows of complete compassion
It is the power to show pity and a forbearance
When those who offend will now comprehend
My scales of justice may sometime do balance
Even gritting my teeth I halted your suffering

GARDENS OF PLENTY AND MASS ABUNDANCE MULTIPLY

I will gather the crop once and many times over as the seeds keep pushing up and the rows multiply
Continual miracle gardens produce in a geometric pattern that has my senses stunned and amazed
The Spirit of abundance has driven the growth axiom to an unlimited harvest I am in perplexed shock
How can the spirit promulgate irrigate and participate in an avalanche of wonderment beyond belief
I am in total awe with a Spirit that gives mass creative abundance before the soul of my eyes unlimited
I will go to the edge of the soil mass and listen to rows of music play as the seeds germinate new life

Whispering My Thoughts

Often we hear ourselves think and hide our thoughts from others around
Sometimes to publish our ideas may lead to a fatal action to our career
The anguish and fury that embraces our thinking is not on printable paper
Hiding our true feelings is an art with balance, finesse and tap dancing
While we are embroiled in a argumentative state we need to look neutral
Others judge us for our masterful avoidance and sheer deflection tactics
We become the most improved propaganda machines without real words
Our ride through the majestic heartland yields patriotic words of compassion
Climb aboard the Washington Express...whisper freedom as your renewal words
A few people may be revitalized and reborn by the message of your fiery eyes

Mystic Tableau

Staring outward is Mendenhall glacier from a Methodist Church in Juneau
Massive reflection of a sky deflection to shine a huge blue ice floe aglow
Appearing as a painting of Van Gogh speaking to me as Henry Thoreau
An artistic arrangement in natures ice plateau mirrors the days shadow
This is a classic of nature's flow allowing me to create a perfect rondeau
Charging onward I understand a massive flambeau creation although
This masterful panorama outflow depicting a beautiful static icicle show
One great spectacle illustrating a hollow frozen arrangement to outgrow
Time will bellow straight as a hedgerow of an artistic quaking bandeau
ign up to sketch the scene in your brain... a rich classic mystic tableau

WISDOM : .... ALIVE IN A CANTICLE OF A JOYFUL FLOWER ARRAYED

Crested around my field of vision the parade of spring colors are arrayed
While I patiently pull out the weeds of life more persistent ones appear
I continually skirmish with all that is foreign in my manicured garden
Rounding my cultivator I will pick my crops and loosen the vagrants
Totally I am encumbered by my focused activity to keep out the briars
Yet in the total march forward briars will continue to reappear in force
My Life work must marshall strength to eradicate life's briars forcefully
Tomorrow will begin a new skirmish I must be a person of great resolve
My mission in life is to keep the roadway clear of clog so I may succeed
Wisdom drives me to defend what I called for.. I will assist in limiting thorns

Massive Turtles

Green Sea turtles abound
Crawling on Oahu beaches
They have massive beauty
Deliberate in their paths
Placid Green Sea turtles
They climb sandy beaches
Angling up the beach they sun themselves as rocks
Without moving they become a treasure of the ocean
Symbols of cautious waiting they are held in esteem
They become a reflection of patient endurance now
Observe the turtles they represent our perseverance

Reigning In the Great Promises

I believed all they told to me as I grew into manhood
Yet there was always some doubts going forward now
It may not be my challenge or great rebellion arising
It may be only that I deduced it was only a statement
While it was only mere words, words held no weight
I went into a world with scars my beliefs were askew
Then Jane Katz opened my door with shock answers
Opening the trivial Gazette was a startling revelation
Ninety five percent of all drivel was just pure opinion
Test words and conclusions:Wisdom outweighs Logic

Pool Fish in Motion

Pools of Koi are fanning their gills
Awaiting for the morning food fest
Gallantly they patiently fan to fan
Waters sparkle as golden to orange
Fantails glimmer and array as day
Amassed numbers have gathered
Timing will show their patience
Waters are glowing in the sun here
A time has arrived to show beauty
All fish compete for beauty shows
Man has devised methods to judge
We appraise the beauty.. too many
Multitudes may change their pools
All revision is a matter of money
Fish change addresses due to sales
Rich clients get to own a best pick
Yet pools will continue to fan all
Fans are energy for crowd pleasers
Fan pools are a patient beauty now
Often are about pompous wealth

Roll At Pearl Harbor

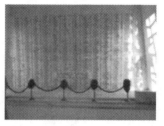

A roll of names I have not heard
I do not know them....I do connect
Repeat names of eleven hundred
It becomes an earth shattering feel
In just a few seconds life changes
All on USS Arizona are casualties
In memoriam say I pray your souls
In Memoriam I saw your courage
In Memoriam I observed silence
In Memoriam I saw your families
In Memoriam we grieve your loss
In Memoriam we will not forget
In Memoriam we listen to taps
In Memoriam we were in oneness
In Memoriam we are proud of you
Ancient Music will play a dirge
All the sadness will rise in oneness
Our Farewell is not goodbye now
Our Farewell sees a new journey
We are comforted by a memorial

Maui Surfers

Today few are riding a pounding surf
Their surfboards are dwarfs in waves
Heads bob up soon covered in swash
Catching a small pipeline a challenge
Bravery is rekindled from the shore
Encouragements now a crowd please
He will stand balance and angle surf
His board makes a statement of him
Rising above water upright gleaming
A young surfer cruises to a shoreline
When focused it appears a young girl
This is not a tomboy but a muscle tot
A well muscled young lady is greeted
She is greeted with an accolade today
The first surfer to make the pipeline
Success is a smiling surfer sailfish
Plow now through water and ask how
Great accomplishment is good timing
Circumstances prevail adapting a key
Prepare yourself and be made aware
Surfer Sandy is focused on elements
Detail elements do surround all of us
How we deal in lifes detail is critical
Plan a planed swath before it happen

Discovering Eros

Isolation can be a mass incident
I can overcome my remoteness
When I clearly say Amen I agree
So often I repeat and then forget
Love I seek internal and external
Reach out and then reach within
Love is a massive embrace of life
Fine tune your gravelly soul self
Arise be enlightened and glow
Our moment in time is very brief
Seek and be a candle for others

Coming to Junctures

There are many doors ahead of me
see choice is a matrix of madness
If I must choose I will be cautious
Junctures can be sharp and cutting
Yet if I study the matrix I succeed
keep focused on all matrix doors
Keep a keen watch on doors above
My bookmind focuses my strength
My heartmind focuses my wisdom
Thoughtfully I align my friendship
Friends I pick are doers and darers
Finding all keys are puzzlebusters
unlock the first opening and test
Testing to retesting breeds success
Life is a continual mass test of all
Utilize my many friends as guides
As I locate keys : I seek journeys
All journeys are testing...be awake
Tomorrow junctures snap.. Ready?

Remembering De Grazia

He carefully sought simple subjects
He used the bri colors on the people
Bringing the highlights of a culture
Using his knives he breathed his life
The American Southwest is an image
Di Grazia's Sombrero with flowers
Horses galloping and tildas angling
Angels playing Violas and smiling
Rodeos rambling with ropes rising
Children playing a fine fiesta dance
Then just a simple Mariachi band

Palo Alto Now

It is labelled Palo Alto right now
It could have been Palo Soprano
Yet it maybe called Palo Tenor
When ground shakes Palo Tremor
Or take flight and see Palo Azul
Deep down inside I see Palo Bass
Of course blinding is Palo Blanco
In a season of Spring is Palo Verde
Could there be several Palos yet
So first I am in need of a song
Palo Alto sing me a song of you

Finding the Masses

Looking outward I see a struggle
There maybe chances for change
Overall a ripple will come initially
Following there is a second wave
Floating in the sands of time hope
Here I see : willing day is working
Here I see : full potential arriving

Following is a third wave I rumble
I am always alive on a third wave
Rumble can turn all upside down
Then hope amazes society as roll
Rumble and roll occur to a replay
All changes will improve my days
Revision becomes a new-key path

My change is mass transformation
I Transform myself in a new mode
Modality arises a pattern behavior
As masses mass into a fine festival
I find life in a fourth wave rising
Festival of life : an innovative path
I locate masses in the fourth wave

Electric Minds

Often I find an electric mind that binds
My memory is watermelon rind of kinds
Then I run behind quite blind to regrinds
Help I am on hinds ready to post reminds
To locate a line... alleviate slime rewinds
Finding electric minds of kinds I realign

Propping Me Up to the Task

Sometimes we find a lifetime void
Arriving at a station we arise to filler
Our emptiness needs to be explored
Critical structures need our attention
We are a complex creation of cells
Filler must be for meaningful masses

Words must align to our rising hope
Emptiness must be more than words
Our action contains : a plain wisdom
Wisdom flourishes and will retrain
Our knowledge revamps and rushes
Wisdom and knowledge succeeds

Prop me up to a task filling emptiness
Voids are difficult to really avoid now
A loss of a loved one is a great space
A change in our status hard to accept
A great separation caused by moving
A great meditation helps an emptiness

The Mystery Man

I saw him arrive on a bicycle with a pack
He was quiet and did not speak English
He was amazed by tables of many items
He finger gestured as to what he wanted
Often very polite and very unassuming
Very intensely he perused the old items
Then knowing his limited bicycle space
He wisely chose a few treasured items
Then knowing his limited purse funds
A decision to round off the dollar totals
He was very happy so too we were happy
So sudden as he had mysteriously arrived
He pedaled at a rapid rate around a way
Then he was gone now in a flurry of time
He was one of a few that stopped today
Our pleasure items was his treasure items
Now he is home exploring his new booty
Hooray for the few that find joy in a hunt

Profound Collaboration

Earth relies on a collaboration of man
Often man turns innovative and careless
Earth needs a gentle touch and adulation
Often man is rough so collectively crude
Earth wants a complete restoration now
Often mans work will revise sky and mud
Earth pleads for its crust cared for gently
Mans obtuseness melts ice caps so drown

Discovering Transformation

The Road to Enlightenment

Cascading in front of us is times voyage through a small opening on a roadbed ahead amassed with wildflowers
Is it possible that I am dreaming or are my feet moving through a trail that appears ahead-Yes I am seeing a path
Crisscrossing the road I see a multitude of paths yet only one is placed on my vision field- a grassy trail upward
Plodding ahead I see a monolith with ancient writing scrolled and there is an eloquent message of real wisdom
"Gather the implements of life and patiently put all structures into spaces of accession grow and be enlightened"

Come to our senses on a warm Spring Morn

All are real excited now
We are set : get a plow
A Spring Season is here
We need to see it clear
Time to plant is a must
In nature we need trust
Our day is now steady

We have become ready : to set our season in prime grow
Carefully and cautiously we mow to plant seeds in a row
Allow for solitary cantata to echo Springs Grand Sonata

Sonnet To Exceptionally Mad Hornets

I woke up early this morning to a loud buzzing clatter
Then I heard an obnoxiously angry cacophony zitting
What could be happening so mad creating such a fitting
I climb onto my corner porch to see what is the matter
A black widow spider is approaching a new hornets nest
All loud buzzing is the the hum roll of warning alarm
Now is the time for it to retreat from this crested farm
Leave or be stung with pointed needles done with a zest
Yet black widow tries a fragile opening space in a cram
Hornets begin deaths formation buzzing an enemy form
Aligning and alighting they prepare to attack like a ram
Flying non stop drop buzzed wings sounding as a storm
Winding and wafting to land a hundred stings in a slam
A poisoned spider is all done hornets remain to reform

Prying the Forest Canopy Open today

Today I see the forest Canopy begin to open and blossom
A colorful array of beauty rises and permeates the land
Today marks the beginning of the new forest covering
Penetration of light is a concentration sight of new arrays
Growth will now announce the new forest configuration
Plans belonged to the Mistress of Nature planning sprigs
Yes blossom sprigs and jutting leaves form natures plan
While I want a part in it : The Grand Uplifting is not min
Roaming into the majestic forest of Nature see a promise
My vision field is aligned with a majestic forest canopy
Today marks a new spring with creations canopy unbrella

Tell and Tell

How we perceive others is a latent force within us that exclaim
We form our thoughts before communicating ..then often empt
Many times our thinking is mulled and skewed without cause
Acceptance of others is a real process of their acceptance of us
If we climb aboard the Universal Cleansing Catalyst right now
Taking action beyond our personal ranking we can rise upright
Cleansing can assist each and every soul by cleaning our parts
Then cleaning a window of our soul can be a beginning action
Our follow up is a mass cleansing on a tell and tell power hose

Burgeoning Forward

I will locate a weak word
A word that seems archai
Take burgeon challenge
I often try to rescue word
Often isolated words live
Some words have homes
Vocabulary can be unique
Today I will be burgeon
Now my exercise is alive

Chautauqua!

I recalled the initial definition
Word of native indian origin
Translate a single meaning of
Forming an American ICON
There is no single translation
For those who inhabit the land
Chautauqua is a form:a way of life
Chautauqua is the lake I fish from
Chautauqua a place where fog is
Chautauqua is a great gathering
Chautauqua is its own geography
Chautauqua is the people residing
Chautauqua is the mystique of it!

Passing Chautauqua is a Portage
This is the route to follow west
An olde French trail route created
A winding pathway to progress
A trek road opening to the West
Here begins a Manifest Destiny?
Allow wagons to traverse inland
People begin a Grand Exploration!

Chautauqua will follow rivers now
Lake Chautauqua runs Chadakoin
Chadakoin runs into Conewango
Conewango runs into Allegheny
Allegheny runs into Mississippi
Mississippi runs into an Atlantic
water my way across the land
Trek canoes to new born vistas
Chautauqua becomes passageways
Pass by land and water routes now
Chatauqua is the stepping point
journey across the frontier miles
You are becoming a Chautauqua!

I see a Chautauqua movement so
Here will commence lyceums now
Educate masses in uplifting music
Propagate the idea of standards
Invent a chorus of deep concern
Lecture those on good and evil
Find a purpose and broadcast it!

Experiencing Dawn

Ahead I observe breaking light
Rays permeate the sky haze here
A half moon dangles in the sky
Before full light begins there is..
There is a short chill then a wind
My eyes see a rising faded blue
Then clouds configure a horizon
A flapping flag informs a storm
Today I will weather all elements
I am the birth of a new tomorrow
If rain will rein today take a drink
Then earth is quenched in puddles
Thus tomorrow grows replenished
Every dawns light writes a story
Always experience:personal dawn

Plying my Way to New Ridge today

My journey is through a Two Way
I need to commence sailing today
A Great Tranquility : a vision day
Across my memory will be a relay
Rounding corners I am here to say
A terrific foresight as I begin play
I will Head to New Ridge as I may
Plying away to be part of a quay
Let me not stop for any real delay
This is a critical race in Tobe bay
Prepare the sails to rip and play
Heavy breezes allow me to sway
Fly on while chasing a manta ray
My Catamaran will lead all spray
I angle the boat so I will not stray
New Ridge champion is my foray

Palominos

I see them from a distant rise now
A Pack of golden horses galloping
Their manes and tails are creme de
Creme de light honey waving hair
Proud of their bay beauty compete
Compete with cleat their light feet
Majestic beats lead a waved parade

Transport to Galaxies

Stellar Nova is a GPF Space Vehicle
Created with lasting point precision
Mapping through outerspace charts
This space vehicle will traverse soon
It will recycle directions to a galaxy
Revisions will be to the nanoseconds
Prepare the androids and all paracells
Journeys are planned for 2318 now
This transport will colonize Bondar
A planet in Galaxy Tretrex Major 1
Our Travel will take 228,000 L Y
We will prepare for mass mutation
Patterns of life will rearrange here

Our objective forms a remote outpost
Bondar will emerge as a new kineses
Our pact is to continue colonization
Our kind will emerge as in mastery
Our Beta impulse is now eliminated
We are descended from a space surge
Space configuration controls ordered
Separation has occured in humanoids
Specific attributes are space ascended
Category Four people are now chosen
Molded from a legacy patterned kind
Category4 can toe rigors in newspace
Prepare: More GPF vehicles readied

The Grand Interlude

A short episode is about to begin here
Forming a consolidated turning point
It unravels quickly as a timed episode
We will embrace this interval briefly
It will be catalogued as critical now
The boulevard of greatness watches
Either this gap filler will be indeliable
Or this dramatic piece will be a flop
Observe this short respite as hopeful
We observe an intermission and look
An interlude remains a potential turn
A great turn to arrange and rearrange
At the intervening turning point a rest
Time will work a small miracle now
The Grand Interlude met its promises
We were refreshed by a flash point
Clamoring for newness we are reborn
Stay mesmerized by a slice in time
Tomorrow we may observe a light
New ideas emblazoned our vision
Celebrate a creative energy moving!

43

Souls On Fire

Observe that we will take all handouts that are offered to us on Monday morning
If we stop and assess the reasons we take...in retrospect it is not need but greed
Our soul when it is on fire... moves when we are burning to reach out to others
Our needs take a back seat to the real reality of destitution and multiple sorrow
To be souls on fire is being transformed to next levels of massive aid and assistance

Your Soul Injected

Loneliness may exist for a season for my own soul in patient waiting
No matter how I view life soul matters in all my situations given
Times of happiness and adversity will arrive at the door of my soul
Times of wholeness and holiness surround my soul infinitely now
Times of wealth and destitution fall upon my soul in circumstance
Souls journey will encompass joy, flatness and many disappointments
A great treasure of my soul is prayer.. it opens hearts to lift emptiness
My soul needs to be in sharing and sometimes in suffering solitude
Sympathetic soul joins others to share the wonders of peace and love

Your Soul Perfected

Passing through the river of life your soul now will arise for eternity
Your soul transcends the surrounding darkness remains free from peril
It resists the brainwashing banners that try to lure your soul to death
You are given free will to exercise a compassion in your heart to others
Magnified by ten dimensions your soul was anointed with discernment
Your soul is your built in direction finder for your lifes complete work
Soul is the capstone of your existence navigating the passages of life
Soul contains the source of your unique purpose to calibrate all details
Soul contains the maps and charts for the several tomorrows to come
Revel in the powerful soul gift you have to experience all creation

Your Soul Elected

A sequel to soul forming is to carry on a mission of ultimate compassion
Here is a milepost of information for us to discover and deseminate now
Our soul becomes educated by the truth that permeates the landscape
Our soul becomes uplifted by the grand beacon that enlightens the way
Once we are elected we cannot allow the secular logic and verbiage in
Power and performance in life requires a souls wholeness and oneness
Our soul is elected to the truth and constantly sets captives free forever
The march to clarity is the march to true charity and real open freedom
Soul is encapsulated in the words of truth and compelled to understand
Soul is the sounding board of our lives journey to assist others in need

Set forth a beautiful Image

We all adorn an image of those so beautiful and pleasant in their appeal
Yet we understand that wear of ages can diminish their glamour at now
Find your mainstream pulse and be comfortable with the self you are
The ravages of time's hourglass will sift then and catch up to all of us
Think of a true time in which our presence was a honored moment
A fruitful moment in times vast tunnel of everlasting Iris blossom
We remain a piece and part of humanities planned great spring outward
Remember your place and time in the massive parade that is forming
All images are in favor with the great creator that formed each of them
Once we understand the phrase 'GOD is LOVE' nothing else matters

Finding Our Challenge

any offer a flower to spring your compassion to their multi level just cause that is sitting on a horizon ahead
ou need to understand that many people use their influence to justify their reason for being and convince you
and up and pay attention to a message... they are blasting the power of their position to brain wash your mind
y self reliance leads me to understand the difference between influence and stating the actual facts as given
se up... brandish the truth... set a podium on fire... truth is a blazing flame that engulfs all the phony phantoms

Racing Toward Avalon

m transfixed and unable to connect all dots I need to complete for technical tasks which I am quickly racing forward on
any times I have relied on others to provide the impetus to build or assemble the precise configuration needed to finish
ow I languish thinking of my part, so now I am alone, thus it has to be self reliance to arrive at a final completion ahead
rected and somewhat perfected the mass project has been completed, I called it AVALON after a beach I once knew
valon is the space vehicle that will thrust the masses of humanity to Planet Cephanoba found in the Magnifest Universe

The Fountain of Lions Beckons me

At the near corner of my eye I see a rising flow of water held by a sentry of lions
I cannot resist the the challenge to quench my parched throat and recurring thirst
Forward I move cautiously and carefully allowing the carnivores their duty station
While the wind works a miracle I stand close enough to enjoy the whiplash spray
Then I place a cup on a stick to reach the flowing fountain from a precipice above
Carefully the bamboo stick allows the cup to dip under and fill overflowing now
Help is the obtuse method devised to save myself from the devouring pride below
Cunning is the catapulting message of life in the stealing seconds of my survival

Find the Right Combinations

e spend too much time on making trite decisions that do little to effect the long and short of our arduous lifes journey
altzing through the thousand doors on the majestic pathway that opens before us is the challenge to make simplicity
sing to the edges we make decisions that make us feel so comfortable and these small decisions appear so important
nen render your life on a calendar and observe how little these trite decisions did nothing to impact your magnus opus

Midnight Butterfly Settling Upon a Butterfly Bush

Oh I see a flower unfold
Midnight butterfly lands
As the Cape winds blow
A seductive aroma draws
I see multitudes of wings
Midnight butterflies land
Amass of them alight to brittle butterfly bush branch
Coloring the bush with a regal magnificence flapping
Now I see an aromatic draw I am tranced by wings

Never have the bounty of butterflies been so abundant
Truly the sensuous smells and odors rise to attract all
My lavender bush remains a stealth of midnight light
Observe the busy wings of creation flapping this epic
My escape from the netherworld is with perfect flight
My ebony will camouflage me in a density of my life
Primary odors have drawn me to this lavender nectar
As the oozing nectar drips I will revel in great delight
The life pattern of my existence may be only 3 month
I will color the countryside with my pattern color win
I will incessantly flap to allow winds blow my take ot
In the quiet moments of tomorrow I crash into eternit

Buttermilk Bay

Fiery sunset lays a rose to my horizon
Reflections on a bay proves its glow
Rosette streaks through these clouds
A red picture paints a celestial sphere
My eyes observe a two tone sky haze
I cannot forget this one August image

Buttermilk Bay can give you a trance
Your focus may create a vivid trace
After days passage red remembrances
Colors can remain in your souls recall
Events do recoil around my memory
Some pleasantries in lifes color image

For a few quiet moments a sun fades
After the final flickers.. darkness sets
Tomorrow I stand on the same ground
A new light projects itself so quickly
My hope of the new day is new light
Buttermilk Bay projects a rose hope

Then evening arrives I do see sunset
Yet this Rose horizon revises slightly
New sunsets do create new memories

Quivet Walking Trail

Along the Cape Cod Bay trails nestle
Two sisters walk a green beach path
Overgrowth is the good shade cover
Toe allows a private nature excursion
Moving swiftly we can catch the tide
Eel grass with tickle our toes and feet
Aligning in sea waters heal our cuts
Aligning in a sea water refreshes us
We will pick beach plums and be full
Then we will crowd a beach umbrella
Staying near a bay makes an appetite
We devour more berries and plums
As a day wears our tide will depart
Charging onward we begin to leave
Heat and sun rays quicken our pace
Other new needs are settling on us
Several trails may beckon us home
Our journey tells us the quicken way
Covering ourselves to avoid insects
We focus on the two new commands
We will locate our new agenda path
We do find our next best move back
Our trail is a daily nature commune

Taughonnock Falls

Gushing down sides of high steep cliffs
Water flows as exciting streams of begin
Begin notes the joining to greater rivers
Massive streams of water roar into pools
Thunder of falls is deafening in our ears
We stand and observe fine sprays rising
We stand in the pools in relief of the hea
Then soon after a stream winds and race

Refreshed and renewed water gives life
Ice cold streams rejeuvenate our bodies
Ancient tributaries flow thru country lan
Creating a pathway they ribbon onward
As a stream flows it seeks other streams
Joining and revving abound into rivers
Rivers may rush as they are conjoin into
Conjoined small rivers drive incessantly

Our watershed is a lifeblood of overflow
Our watershed is a drought of underflow
We are powerless to predict the waterfal
Taughonnock is our all measuring baske
Our souls can predict the river by a falls
The harder a falls blasts over these edge
Greater will be the flood plains below us
Taughonnock hold back your rage quiet

Bridging all the Gaps

All the great ideas of man are compullated and rigorously evaluated in the annals of times significant moments
Hashing and rehashing how man has handled himself in stress and discomfort then in ease and great pleasantry
Man is not the measure of all things but a critical part of the grand design epic of our long civilized earthly rise
In a porous mileau of several centuries new discoveries have made the saga of life very tenuous and very tragic
Man stuggles and wavers to help his fellow man to eliminate gaps yet the gaps are often too significant to fill up
As gaps are measured they are difficult to navigate.. deep to imagine..hard to understand..overwhelming as void
Bridging the gaps is a monumental task too difficult to perform..... likely a huge wall of undefined hard questions
As we go into the twenty second century ...should man survive as an entity... A Gap Institute forms as a Bridge

New Jersey Marshlands

Along the coast path I follow the ribbon trails that hug the coast so close
Mulling through the great marshland tidepools I see life awash in vigor
Through a marshland grass small amoeba swim as a beginning life form
Larger life forms find their meals and a cycle begins:earths life hierarchy
New Jersey earth man has been a fortunate inhabitant of the beginnings
A trellis of green grass forms a photosynthesis sea garden of life longing
An amazing carpet of green trails a coastline creating my miracle miles
Tomorrow I will discover a green revolution formed to keep us so clean
New Jersey Marshlands breathe a breath of lifes origins as a continuity
As I continue my vigilant walk I realize the abundance of this creation

Cape May Beach fence

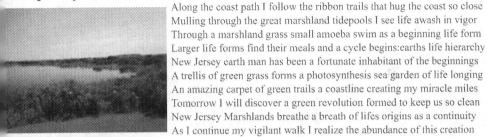

A weather beaten and battered fence reminds me of the great hurricane
How the tremendous forces of nature prevail upon open seascape lands
I see the pillaged beach sands and in time the wind whips so incessantly
Sea grass and sea reeds hold some of Cape May together in the battering
At a distance a great Sea Cottage remains upright as an old tested edifice
Reigning down the coast this fence remains as a testament of wired hope
My sea fence was weathered but holds steady as my New Jersey friends
I will rise tomorrow morning to wash clapboards on gingerbread houses
The many colors on the lanes and street remain a brilliant bound bastion
My heart revers into the strength of beach fences and Cape May courage

One of 1863 ISLANDS

One solitary island builds a story of terminal morass delta sand and rock
Just one lonely uninhabited isolated spot can recall this constant buildup
The Saint Lawrence flows with a rush of the time and tide pouring on
Eventually passing from Lake Ontario it becomes a mass feeder stream
Our Saint Lawrence constantly pushes on the geography of the islands
Formations begin and end in the weathering and rush of this great river
Clamoring onward it is hard for us to fathom counting Thousand Islands
Where do I begin and settle and what small rise constitutes a real island
Masses of literature explain what an island is and how to explore its area
Define the number of rises in this island chain as gifts of Saint Lawrence

Defined Tomorrow

My life is a validation of
many years concentration
I worked and had impact
on a significant yesterday
I carefully built structures
These edifices were completed to assure my survival
Concentrating on a whole self... I circled my family
All the sound structures remained as building blocks
Tomorrow I go and define the many futures waiting

Trace and Track

Going forward I see hard choices... trace and track
Many times I called for assistance...trace and track
In several instances I made moves..trace and track
I will be judged by my finesse....trace and track
Now I will trace and track my total pathway map
Trace and track the essence of all my quick thoughts
Trace and track a continuous flow of life's memories
Trace the good times...track all the marginal endings
My balance sheet reads a positive eternal message
Complaint not part of my vocabulary, how about you?

Remembering Muir Woods

John Muir was an astute young man
He saw untainted beauty to capture
His target was preserve national gems
John was an ardent lover of nature
Sharing his thoughts was to influence
Johns actions were very well defined
Preserve natures beauty for all to see
Strong will was his character defect
Converting others to preserving a key
He formed a network with a passion
Announcing needs was a proliferation
With action he formed green groups
Nature was in need of great protectors
John Muir was Natures Conservator
His friends saw his great mission now
Aiming is to keep the landscape alive
With few assets and much free effort
John Muir has saved the countryside
John Muir has breathed life in forests
We named a plot of land Muir Woods
In all its glory it is a tribute to visions
Visionaries spot the land in revival
The Revival is a make clear for ages
Celebrate the redwoods in awe now

Attacking My Apathy

Time lag and weariness is a crutch
It is a frontal attack on ambition
Many times people are left waiting
Compatriot wait a disappointment
When the bell of 'to do' rings now
Action is not at the top of my list
My internal clock is running fast
I do need to regroup to get started
I will begin a brand new invective
I will be more urgently motivated
I will consider the plight of others
I will begin to see a total picture
An hour glass of sand is driving
Thus I must be way more attentive
Fix my breath and remember need
Action will bury continued apathy
Find a broken bridge and repair it
Find a broken person and remold
Remold parts and provide a path

MELLOW MINDSET

I sit on an airport bench waiting departur
I continue hearing of my flight delays
Changes will direct to miss the dart mark
The board keeps generating ten message
No comments are soothing or warning

I need to get home now it broke my hear
Mindless and hopeless are the messages
Can they get this altogether and take off
We sit grounded like a pound of hambur

I cannot control any shaky airport events
I will sit and remain in ominous restraint
Smiling and real mellow I appear calm
Then I take a breather and wheel a cart

Hope is to see a powerful flashing word
Yet time is overwhelming my senses
I know I am overburdened and excitable
Yet I will do my part and fall into line

Trying to get home I try changing flights
All flights are full and I am frozen now
I must retain a mellow mindset for this
Anger is the flame thrower that burns m

Black Mourning

Sorrow creeps in very quickly
It can destroy our crested hope
Gradually small factors combine
Giving us our great depression

Once the great light diminishes
We soon seize the last few rays
Stuffing a glow into our pockets
Our vision becomes total ebony

On a new mourning we will cry
Once a sudden death has passed
We will open our pockets again
Black mourning will vaporize

A new horizon will beam aloft
Black mourning passed slowly
New rays move at a low tangent
will arise and bathe in its light

Day Comes to Us Dressed Up in Total Mass Illusion

Break of day often changes radically
Ultimately the sun drops out of sight
Unassumingly clouds gather a thunder
Rapidly gray amasses in the whole sky
Razor lightening strikes in many places
Torrents of rain drive wild streams aloof
Our shoreline overflows with vengeance
Our land mass revises with raging waters
Floods drive through the open lowlands
A momentary burst caves an earthen dam
Tomorrow will capture the lands renewal
Lands perimeters changes our geography
A revised map redefines all outer edges

Rushing to the floral Wonder Untamed

Spring lazes back and finally explodes
It will meander then dresses when ready
Spring sends a full bonfire of blossoms
All renewal prepares for the strong winds
Change baptizes the land with wild rains
Suddenly a second rage of color bursts
A whole countryside amasses in radiance
Paint me refreshing rushing floral wonder
Spring sprung a untamed renamed flame

SINGULAR

Rushing into a new concept can be insane
Yet sometimes life can leave us very flat
Charging ahead we see a vibrant newness
Making a movement seems to be correct
Bravery is the keynote of our action now
Tomorrow our singular solar panel comes
Our brain will run on single solar power

Home is a Springboard

Gathering mass speed bits of information
Is grafting power into a concept as a plan
All plans are shuttled on the first pathway
Structuring is acorn ideas to critical paths
We sort out paths to current end matrices
Our lives will settle and resettle in matrix
This translates that a home is a good start
Yet you are never home until a movement
When our springboard moves you arrive
Observe springboards move bound paths
New plans will spring us to new heights

Fair the Midland

At times it is the mediocre way I do feel
This an experience of flatness without joy
Warm elation minus no follow through
Seeing others taking them as stale bread
Choosing a flat highway devoid of curves
Rolling forward and laying down prone
Rising to an occasion and barely smiling
Allowing for just a few of lifes pleasures
Overwhelmed and just.... fair the midland

I Now Know My Doggeral

There is a pithy path of promotion here
All drawn divas will look elegent shining
Tracing limelights is a key time at center
Seeking notice and applause constantly
Drawing promptly fast focus at mid stage
Rough edges disappear so we act haughty
We relive an opportunity take centerstage
Then an internal windstorm replaces us
Yes now in walks Dan Doggeral himself

Sunrise on Cape Cod

I see it arrive as a sudden rolling orange
Appearing on a flat hazy Cape horizon
From East Dennis I see Provincetown
At a distance a dedicated pilgrim tower
An early landing encounter on a beach
In winters setting all appeared very bleak
How pilgrims survive: a horizon miracle
Current sunrises contain a subtle breeze
I sense a glow of wealth and opulence
Later a Gulf Stream storm changes all

Address Book

Names reside inside my address applied
People collide with those who have died
Keeping rawhide inside I often confide
Do I keep stride with those on Edens ride
Or may I address all supplied spirit pride
To finally be on a side that changed a tide

Climbing With a Bannister

Climbing out of my very deep concrete cellar
Often my stride was with no firm place holder
When a friend kindly had a thought real stellar
Perhaps a suggestion which was quite bolder

You might align stairs with several cannisters
This may give you a grip that helps the rise
Then I thought why not look at two bannisters
I had the grips installed much to my surprise

Bannisters were answers to my great chagrin
Next time I think I will swallow a safety pin
Great thinkers may think my brain was akin
Rising out in time : a massive raised ice bin

Playing a game of Street Ball

When the time came to invent we needed balls
Our games were simple we had no game halls
Foremost we had time.. we invented wingfalls
When a player is up one pitch to hit be smalls
Either golf it swat it until Kingdom come calls
Keep our heads up to run as if chasing squalls
Once we got started we would have no stalls
We created fun as our unending untimed malls

Memorablia

We collect our hobby with a powerful passion
Something inside of us will fill our great need
It continues unabated to want more and more
Our grand collection becomes an historic one
Many devouring dealers chase us as one prize
As last breath draws near us vultures multiply
Our grand horde of happiness will be split up
There was no room on deaths chariot for this

Sensational

Often there is no one word that describes hope
Often there is no one word that describes pope
Often there is no one word that describes cope
Often there is no one word that describes rope

Pope unties rope allows you to cope with hope

Drifting to Reykjavik

In my long travels my boat drifts past icebergs
I see a prism through these dense ice patterns
Many colored facets are meticulously blinding
My craft drifts in the sea avoiding a collision
Without sight without direction I am so adrift
A great ocean liner sends a signal of distress
Small fishing boats soon surround my old soul
The iceman of Reykjavik rescue my old boat
As more icebergs pass my small craft I gaze
A toe line is attached to my boat De Baroque
Now I will go to the safe harbor of Reykjavik
Here I will observe the mystical ice patterns
Safely I do witness a mass of ice prism colors

WATCHING THE WAVES CRASH

Slowly and intensely a rising surf pounds incessantly on a beach at Chatham Cove as a storm now approaches
As all marine life has adapted to the waves of natures calling now a new episode for sea life is about to churn
A maddening Nor Easter aimed at our shoreline will soon begin its intended havoc as it begins to rise quickly
In a sudden second a rollicking wind hits the shoreline blowing hard and topples two maples at beach cove end
Then the surf rolls heavy and crashes in multiple sequences at the shoreline edge creating a vicious undertow
The small sea life is now being pummeled at an alarming rate and must creep or crawl to small islands of safety
Tomorrow as a surf subsides remains of all sea life who perished will be swept up by eager armies of sea gulls

Separation Bridge

Once perhaps ....only a few moments in times window bullets whizzed
Only a Separation Bridge hid the reasons for impersonal angry conflict
In times void we may lose track of our hate and rampent disfigurement
Perhaps all the hollow reasons will accumulate on paper and in words
In the end it will once again measure mans brutal inhumanity to man
We cannot restore the maimed and dead to give just cause for our deeds
As the water passes through the Shannon, Corrib and several other river
Allow the waters to wash away the hate and the fiery altercations abrew
Then allow a healing moment transpire across the connecting bridges
Reconnect on the Separation Bridge and rename it Total Amelioration

Entre to Saint Kevins

Rising on a purple June morning I see the great Saint Kevin Monastery
Passing through the entree not a stone moved nor a wall did collapse
How the ancients conceived how an architecture would withstand time
Arriving through an arched gate I reflect on a welcoming bound beauty
My personage is aglow in a Glendalough countryside that surrounds me
As I walk through this ancient edifice I am lifted up by a rising tower
Great green garrolous pathways lead as a stepping stone in the heavens
I will write my friends of this enchanted experience....they may enjoy
Now as my short trip is unraveling.. the a time of my Irish visit is endin
Passively I am locked in a verdant wonderment a pleasant green ecstasy

Crashing on the Irish West Coast

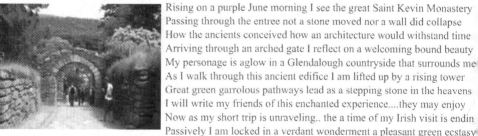

I see the fury of the ancient sea as it quickly whips waves in sequences
Maddening clouds and renegade winds rip their natural forces on land
I observe the green carpet covering shivering as it leeches the sky water
Rolling forward my eyes perceive a natural coastal washing and rinsing
Cycles occur and re-cccur to create a rolling image etched in my mind
From a distance a sea meets the land and greets it with moss green hand
Splashing occurs as a continual celebration to represent a new agreemer
Lashing winds force the clouds to spew massive sprays of water around
Sea water and rain water intermingle to create a defined carpets edge
While the remaining sheets of rain create squalls on the Irish West Coas

50

Standing in a Pavilion

Our magnet Pavilion is constructed
We were aghast at its mass dimension
It was a mass collaboration by many
It is a handiwork of rising multitudes
A Grand Pavilion reaches all heavens
It is not exclusive but rather inclusive
Arise to form a prayer of completion
True believers will stand on the inside
Bellowing words resonate on walls
Echoes of remembrance are calling
Simplicity is difficult in complexity
Transition complexity to small words
Utter the eternal promise I Believe
Fall on your knees horsemen cometh
They will take you up to the parapet
Arise and see a Pavilion of Promise
All Promise Keepers come for you

Reliable

She was always there for me in need
There was no trumpets to remind her
Gently she cared for all my directions
Carefully put the days plans in place
Leered upon my true overall attitudes
She was there to correct my failures
Using words-you better pay attention

She did not accept half -heartedness
And the mother of prime invention
She helped you survive the turmoil
Stop cold- did you ever say thank you
She is remembered in all your actions
Rise up give your mother applause
She is your greatest reliable supporter

Complex Interlude

Magnificent meetings lead to conclusions
Fascinating accomplishment is expansive
Discovering new unrestrictive pathways
All this challenge leads to a breakthrough
Our universe moves at phenomenal speed
Obsessed with remarkable acceleration
Smiling we travel at unrestrictive speeds
We explore a massive complex interlude
Our traveling is forming great blue shifts
Many of us break off into smaller drifts
Uncovering our lives mission we focus
Zero in on the details of our quick lives
Locate the passion fruit of our laboring
Tomorrow we re-assess our Zip Speed
Our quick decision making yields results
We are the mutants that travel in travail
We do not really have a home base path
Our future is a new Complex Interlude
resting place when we run out of fuel

Mass Clusters Collectively Colliding

Motion in luminescent universe complex
Laws of man define and explain all space
Space is an ever expanding illusion for us
Mans law cannot apply in lightyear space
Consider galaxies may cross pathways
Sudden robust discoveries are uncovered
Countless collisions occur in gravity field
Then obtuse actions deliver energy bursts
Mind boggling change to scientific paper
Restoration words deliver new reactions
Some scientists reject new re-executions
Space travelers reflect calm and concern
Space leadership marked by sober intent
Several extraordinary passages redone
Great cluster remain intact some collide
Some new collisions remain unexplained
Man struggles to define multi-universes

Enlightened Way

Once I discovered an Enlightened Garden
Placid man of quiet wisdom spoke to me
Wisdom was his treasured gift to delight
All endowments of magnificence reside

Enlightened Garden come to me again
So I might bathe in your total serenity

Quaking in the Verbal Abuse

Often we are taken and slighted about
Those who are our allies are Battlers
They will often even turn to do battle
Pinions of arrows are painful reminders
War whoops are contagious cacophony
Final screams are plentiful and will echo
A constant echo reminds us to pace quiet
Quiet pacing can confuse the pursuers
You may have set up an unknown barrier

Those who are allies are sometimes foes
They creep in your conscience enmasse
Remember to give the screamers space
Space at the table and at the conversation
When a bugle does call keep composure
A battle has already been fought and won
Wave to a crowd and hold your one head
Tomorrow your smile wins over enemies
Quaking will not occur until after prayer

Camp at the Rim

Finding a proper campsite is a challenge
First scoping out an area for soft needles
Second carefully look for cover or shade
Third find latrine areas are sane and safe
Finally locate a sane camper to get sleep
Allow the big moon to shed light after ten
We rest in our sleeping bag until til morn

Aligning Next Years Garden

Our memory can often be very shallow
In fact it unremembers what planted last
In a grid given pattern seeds were sown
Every year changes occur to fertile land
Replenish the nutrients and mulch it all
Memories may fade between years now
Yet the land knows what it needs to grow

Every year I draw the pattern on patterns
Rotating my A wheel of seed to a pattern
The A wheel tells what is in need indeed
Certain seed has certain real soil flavors
Spinach does not like La coffee grounds
Peas want always their Pea fence moved
Carrots spoil and do not like alkaline soil

I uplift my mindset to a constant change
The desert has one winter growing season
Get my hands moving fast in late October
Find a delicious mulch mix combination
Get all the oozing coffee and tea grounds
Water lands and hope for the earthworms
Sow seed multitude upon quiet landscape

Stand back slowly--yell grow Grow grow

Durango Silverton

How can you never remember the ride
In open crate car an engine smoke chokes
Those enclosed did miss the countryside
We saw marvelous Colorado mountains
The ride was an icy cold August morning
Does it ever get warm in mountain peaks
Maybe one day in real late August heat

Chugging across a land the whistle blew
The sound sent twelve deer running fast
They galloped as a spooked horse herd
Yet as they disappeared loose rocks fell
What fell was undiscovered out of sight
Our train constantly is rounding bends
Moving through passes of least obstacles

Finding the Durango Silverton iron horse
This is an adventure in southwest history
Our trains run on the mountain and plains
Pushing new civilizations to a mass cut
As they cut through crevices and drive
The driven were digging for gold riches
All that remains is trains and the whistles

Chugging is a sound of click-clack tracks
The Iron horse pounds around the rocks
We take a picture of the purple mountains
Our journey runs quick in the afternoons
We soon chug to Silverton all train crazed

51

Answering The Mass Mailings

Some souls need paper mail
Often they mail to get mail
Loneliness is an escape to
If I receive I am a persona
A Key Mission is analysis
What will some other sources send me for allegiance
Will they give me free tickets or food or false hope
Yet at a minimum they will send me tickets to pass A
Here I will be given Pass A treatment to spend dollars
Pass A is a destination with my checkbook as hostage

As I become wrapped in Mass mailing a mind breaks
I cannot remember who gave me the license to fish
Constantly I am enmeshed fishing for great deals now
No real promise in an avalanche of my mass mailings
My faltering fishing experience has left me exhausted
Soon the merry moochers of Moonville come calling
I get personal treatment at my lighthouse entrance
They will deliver groceries gifts and gratitude here
I am wowed by the all personal attention given to me
Shifting gears to save my integrity I need to say NO
Several tintilating talkers time their marketing blurbs
Tomorrow I unplug phones change addresses.. Poof!

Comb Coquille beach

Drifting at Coquille driftwood abounds
At all my minions are pieces and stumps
Vigorous storms released sea trees here
Now a beach has become a depository
Slashing winds and winter storms clash
The sides of hills erode and trees collapse
Rolling waves and sharp beach monoliths
Times waves create a wood soup arriving
A whole shoreline crowded with debris
Souvenirs of Oregon available to carve
Perhaps a wood fire on the beach now
Then again there is great art to consider
Masses of wood can create a homeyness
Perhaps the beach may need a gathering
There must be a reason for wood float
May it create homes for sea creatures
May it provide wood for sea bird nests
May it allow for paths for beachcombers
May it contain the spring tides arriving
May it show treasure hunters a course
May it stumble those who invade sea life

Mostly I see natural culls of natures work
The handicraft of times beach evolution
Works that man did not create in mind
Carving of a greater force than mankind

Rhyme My Thyme

Many events may occur in peak time
Pictures reinvent my wilderness story
How a June snow wiped out my trek
Master blizzards pasted in new rhyme
Nature wins some of these in glory
No sorrow is shed for snows wreck

Patiently I await early July meltdown
Then I will proceed to a showdown
Will it melt so I see a ground brown
Maybe I will wait wearing a ice crown
Yet when I least expect from uptown
Massive plows remove snow is blown

Now I will take the allotted true time
Mimicking I create a bold pantomime
I ice-race life becoming truly sublime
Wearing snow masks I hide my crime
Snow dancing I will stop on a dime
Really my thoughts are far too prime

Now I will climb a rhyme in my time
Running up a slush hill in snow slime

Freedoms Voices

Rushing waters pour through my brain
As they cascade around corners they fly
Often I hear flowing... my life's waterfall
It must be the brain cells translating all
Powerful messages are digested and dry
Dry messages charge with a water spray
Multitudes of words are given a purpose
A running river of words gives us choice
I make efforts to swallow my own pride
Some messages are not accepted well ye
As I delve into the future I listen clearly
Being attentive may allow good growth
The rumbling wash of words are bisecte
While I know I divert some key message
My heart and soul require my acceptance

The flow of life makes me very cautious
Ancient rivers dwell to refresh my brain
Constant to careful decisions bloom now
I become awash in ideas about freedom
Hearing the unabashed truth can shake
Our whole being needs a chinking chain
Yet the river does not chink it cascades
I need to run with Freedom River aloud
Sound of the rushing water speaks to me
I must follow the Freedom rush or drow

52

Digging the Party Worms

Collectively I sit pondering worms
Our party is going angling later
What juicy worms are available
Can I attract a huge Lake Trout
Can I quickly provide a winner
Night Crawlers are the best bet
I need to be deep digging in mulch
I need fresh rotting mulch abound
Find the soft stinky piles of ripe
Find the crawl and squirm babies
Capture them in a ball of seaweed
Find safe refrigerator crawl spaces
Tomorrow I cast my fate in ponds

Giving Becomes Living

Having it all and then some is not living
Our small brains need not acquire hoards
Stepping forward we free ourselves soon
Soon we stuff vehicles with excess goods
What we cannot use must be released
Chariots may come unannounced waiting
Our largess must be now to help agencies
Those suffering can be relieved at once
Our meagre assets are employed to save
Find room in your soul to release wealth
Swing low, it is all a temporary benefit
Open the eyes of your heart and give
A flow of excess will transition your soul
Tomorrow you will be released and free
Bondage is not the goal of living things

Accept your Status

I am who I am in forever time
Should the directions change over
Adjust my thoughts and purpose
Yet my sum physiognomy remains
Finite revision does not alter me
Everyones opinion fixed as fossils
My imprint was made in stone
Carefully observe your reforming
Tomorrow you are not recognized
Remember to leave fossil remains
We are here for short denouements
Prepare my statement a fulfillment
I am a man without a ruling status
I focus on a next order from above
My status declared by acceptance

Bellowing through the Republic

Travel across this fifty star republic
Colorful images arise on each horizon
Each starred state has its own persona
I bellow my loudest as each unfolds
All demonstrations of unique sources
I must be amazed at slight differences

It is the peace of the people as distinct
It is the contour of landscape differs
It is structures surrounding unique
It is the vegetation growing clusters
It is the roads that weave in the land
It is the cultural celebrations ringing
It is the native animals in habitation
It is how morning sunrises six sharp
It is a state flag making a statement
It is the historic elements that survive
It is the grandeur of the local color
It is the courage of a chosen few
It is the charm that speaks rural truth
It is you and I having a local chitchat

Most importantly it is regional pride
A smiling pride says I am who I am

Continuity

Following the circular path I am bound
My steps are carefully droned in cadence
The same trail markers repeat and repeat
Some parts of my life repetitious as this
My task is to keep wiry high energy busy
Trekking in given circles drive continuity
I will encompass twenty continuations
Maybe the same circle is significant now
Perhaps repetition is sign in life's journey
My grandchildren unaware of repetition
They know that some animals reappear
We have completed our trip to the zoo
Tomorrow the lion roars twenty times
Tomorrow twenty times at someone else.

Energize the Day's Journey

After I wake in the morning sun glare
My face is drenched with sweat drips
Containing myself I realize no air is on
This is a rising to immediate showers
I need to be fully together to function
Desert heat can broil your body parts
Relief becomes an immediate essential
Sonoran sunrise in the summer is hot
Lubricate with water to keep a bit alive
Today may be a great thirst challenge
Keep the journey energized and full

Adventure is Arising at BEX

Patterns upon patterns appear where
they were totally unexpected
Inconsistencies gradually surround
my magnetic matrix pathway
Flowing in a specific direction I still
see positive movements
Explanation will require heavy
analysis before certain chaos appears
I will take direct actions to swiftly
pinpoint issues to amend anomalies
Several patterns present a logic soon
to morph into a mired illogic
Persevering I follow a magnetic track
to find an effective solution
I goal to locate the several hellion
matrices for my project XXV

A code analysis is now filtering
to create a final patterned solution
First X is the forward doorway code
to the Galaxy ship HEXUS
Second X is the light year speed to
arrive at the planet Bondewea X
My V is the required velocity I must
achieve to break through the
Magnetic Matrix Moving above
Survival Station BEX

Charge to Percussion Drum Beats

There is a cadence that is familiar
Percussion drums roll their slickstix
I am kept awake by the persistent tick
Molded to create an awesome beat
Listen to the echo that fills a stadium
A formation moves in a unison march
Now a rising crescendo blasts away
See a disciplined brass embolden now
In the back hear the whirling sounds
I pick up on blare sounds of crickets
It is the sure purring whirring majesty
As a band marches forward in jettison
Several other instruments joining us
Rejoicing Drum majorettes kick high
We are the toast of bellowing crowds
Arise to the wonderment of parades
Keep the rolling beats going forward
Penetrate the day with vim and verve
We have been thoroughly percussed

Lowville

Steaming through Lowville and passing across the land of continuous roll over hills formed by the ice glaciers
I remain complacent in an olive drab truck listening to the clickity clack clickity concrete roadbed singing to me
On the roadside I see an old farmhouse in decay soon followed by others in freshly painted rich barn red beauty
How I perceive the frame of the landscape in its majesty with the sound of heavy tractors aerating the low fields
Amazed I have done this trip five times before and I remember narrow roads and tight surroundings with fences
Yes and I recall an ancient New York Nightingale song filling my air in time and toil with cool breezes blowing
A clickity clack road muses through its smallness and togetherness in a compact complete low humming tone
Memory also draws a picture of a beaming farm girl trudging late across a few remaining acres in a jeep jalopy
So we begin to understand the rectangular tracts that feed the multitudes belong to little people on little plots
Then I rise up on my journey I wave a great thanksgiving for Lowville the people who find a love for this land

Meaning of the Seven Attitudes

Yes I have read in great Revelation how our seven attitudes shape a verbal landscape with catastrophic meaning
I wrote about all connecting lines and unconstrained thoughts measuring how attitude shapes our commitment
A host of mainstream thinking causes anguish among believers because it strays into a barren boondoggle field
Weak thinking and action amasses my human weakness and it dislocates my wisdom and replaces it with logic
Logic has its place in measurement and mechanics but it becomes stale bread to a great army of true believers
My attitude at Ephesus and my great lack of fervor and absence of patient endurance made me fail to be rooted
Then I walked further into Smyrna and I recognized I could not accept the need for purity and my afflictions
I left and journeyed to my Pergamum and found my life totally wrapped up and gyrating in a group of serpents
So then I scurried onward and awkward to Thyatra to worship the great false attitudes of the rising secular city
Walking quicker I arrived at Sardis and tired I fell asleep and found that as I woke I was unprepared to do battle
At that point I was fleeing I Arrived in Philadelphia and awaiting a miracle but my open door closed abruptly
My last hope racing to Laodocea I dreamed but as I moved I became lukewarm and weak kneed and caved in
Then I saw a vision ahead and realized I was unfocused and not useful and spewed out in a massive manner
Commitment carries a great cost in friendship and aliveness in the spirit of transition and traceability forever
Our attitudes precede us and need to be sharpened to be of any use to the standing army of true blue believers

Lopsided

Several times I have observed how amazing our life works in general, then how people control others thinking
Perceiving through the hour glass running : Controllers believe and think all their singular opinion should rule
Control is the mindset of extremism as it extends across our planet to encapsulate and imprison the minds of all
Control magnets try to rule over the masses desiring to manipulate business political and social structures now
Yet I understand time has a way of infiltrating and undermining the controllers ruining their lopsided equation
Yes I am an observer of a total planet obstruction and I watch from a distance as raging rivers wash it all away

Climbing through the Presidio

Pleasant thoughts are communicated as all the landscape is reeling about on a welcoming July afternoon with fog season
Masses of Nasturtium and yellow daisies triumph and below this is a few mounds of San Francisco Lissingia are bursting
Then I see through the Presidio lowlands the marvelous Lobos Creek dunes that project a vivid image of a settled bay are
This must be a picture that Ansel Adams would have taken : then further I know why the native Ohlone came here to hun
Powder blue Dune Gilia array themselves in unison and patiently stand guard over Lobos Head in the mid summer breeze
I observe at seaside the massive native silvery Lupines as they drink a wandering fog mist that drifts to quench their thirst

Goblet of Times Celebration

Raising the Glass of Celebration I see hope here

All who join me are exuberant with peace and joy

Time has arrived to honor the great creators servants

Announce the message of accomplishment to the bearers

In our lifetime we note several outstanding quiet heroes

Rise in the early bleak hours of this morning now

Take special action and propose a toast

Speak a great hurrah for success

Enter Special eloquence

Drink compassion

Believe

Saints

Are

Now

Eternal Wine Goblet Carriers

Magnificence Detected

am planning several events in my upcoming life and have carefully mapped out all the sordid finite details
have painstakingly spelled out all the necessary steps needed to accomplish these specific golden celebrations
have given the special instructions to all the participants that are planning to recite the words of my greatness
have readied the great tents of tenacity to announce my arrival at 4 o'clock ...then at 2 o'clock I passed away

Pepatacalis : Renewable Non-babbling Morass Mouth

rising from the ashes of my accomplishment I gave a critical speech on the the importance of avoiding Pepatacalis now
here were so many critical components essential in avoiding the condition of Pepatacalis that I spent hours listing them
n the first Saturday of the year 2088 I stood before an empty room reciting the warning to all who would listen and heed
received a truckload of empty accolades from many people in distant precincts who somehow heard the warning echoes
was so amazed at the response of multitudes of my fellow human beings I now have concluded that I must write a book
epatacalis is an ancient honorable disease that infects brain strings of all who know a massive nothing about everything
lease help the owners of the Snook Publication Enterprise spread my words in the proper formats to dizzy dome masses

Rescue the Precious Moments

Glory overtakes us and allows us to witness the great luminous lights which radiate out on the trail
Winding up the trail to the summit of the hill powerful luminaries line a perimeter of the switchbacks
I clearly see the direction of deflection which carries me forward to a pinnacle of surrealism's painting
One can barely imagine how Luminaries become precious moments in times capsule enlightenment
Find the capstone of your magnificent experience and paint the words of your vision on papers edges

Blanket Weave

Time arrives and creatively moves to an overdrive compulsion of doing
Then I weave flower beds, I weave a basket, I weave a simple story
Then I weave a computer solution and then I weave a blanket to cover
My cover is part of my continual weave of life's daily circumstances
Over time I am kept warm in truth by the blanket.... stitch by stitch
Every single cloth bit weave by bit is weaved ominously to cover me
I must be overexposed and oversubscribed but the weaves cover me
Keep the blanket weaves in the memory of the multitudes as magical
Take action and send the bristling blankets of Batavia to Bangladesh
Send cranberry red blankets of Bordentown to bleach beaches in Belize

Massive Structures

I see the azure skies beckon me out in the near distance that shape today
Today I will see tasks that I let slide by later taken over then completed
How was it that other marching machines whisked through completion
What I stalled doing was expediently done by neighbors in residence
Lax attitudes and Lax motivation may have a finite cost then tomorrow
I must reinforce the beacon of my brain that failed to guide me forward
Tomorrow the fishing boats dock at Wellfleet I must help unload cargo
Massive structures haul in the catch and we quickly separate all flesh
Some tasks cannot wait for rotting fish flesh becomes very unappealing
Focus on the massive tasks that lie ahead or be consumed by the day

Wavering Ahead

Landscapes present a powerful panorama of entry and reentry in view
How we command the land before us becomes a novel ardent adventure
We train the eye and ear to sense the structures that present an impasse
Then we focus on rugged trails that lie in our path way and trek ahead
No one other than ourselves can witness our personal journey through it
Trudging onward we navigate the land that captures our silent soul now
Many narrow channels and steep switchbacks present a fierce challenge
Yet our mental toughness and forward vision drives us on to New Eden
We will arrive on time to a land of blooming lily pads and Astral Wonder

ARISE QUICKLY

Arise to the Shades of Tomorrows Benediction

If you would listen you might hear the sound of those who cannot observe tomorrows massive benediction
While they can in spirit they cannot arise and walk and relish this with human eyes, ears, noses and sense it
Those of us who can ring the chimes of acceptance and sing the words from the ancient hymnals, rejoice now!
Great bellowing will occur tomorrow morning from the grand organ pipes that permeate the church structure
Arise now and I say again arise to the rush of the musical intonations that fill the the voids in your quiet souls
I say you who are here appreciate the perfect blending of mystical notes that fill the surrounding countryside
Think if tomorrow may be your last day on earth that you were sent a musical bouquet on your day of departure
Find the Grand Chorus and allow them to sing to your heart for the best day should be one of great salutation
Today I will go in preparation for tomorrow I will locate my seat, my instrument and my twelve music sheets
Tomorrow I will arise quickly and find music for twelve apostles and commence singing to raise a benediction

Remembering the day

Patiently walk by the flowered trail ahead
Bounded flowers remind me of accidents
I will attempt to overcome cluttered paths
While I was patient others screamed life
Lazarus was not raised only loud voices
My fear of helplessness prevailed then
Try as want: time to leave was time to go
Settling across the horizon I became still
Suspended animation was the moment
Then as the light prevailed I saw today
Then as darkness remembered yesterday
Raising my eyes of tears I am helpless
I cannot change past: I can paint futures

Recolor my life as a remembrance always

Passionate in my Total Given Worldly Accomplishment

I understand my rocky road approach
I get cold and calculating as an action
How others see me becomes an issue
Roll to observe my plain views lurking

While I know my ideas are not in favor
I plod forward with bag of new thoughts
Arriving at the podium of positivity I call
My call : one of rethinking past pathways
My call : tracing the failure of yesterday
My call : pulling good pieces of old plans
My call : Pinpointing possible new cells
My call : Growing new cells to maturity
My call : Testing and retesting all wonder
My call : Put wonder into other minds

In finality I must be an eloquent author
Passionate ideas can get trip wired fast
Clearly I must be a crusader for newness
New Ideas cause change to consternation
Find and flush a reason for rampant redo
It is not all about world accomplishment
It is tracing evolved pathways to truth

Bending the Fastidious Rules

Hammered into our soul are the rule to go
We are constantly mapping all truth trails
Testing can arise at any moment from all
All will analyze our actions and motives
Did we have best interests on our minds
They will then measure your hearts first
Hearts are read an then compliance tested
Were you really on page one for cause
Our intentions are constantly tested now
Be seekers of true answers to true colors
We are the only banners flying in peace
Rules can be bent to favor a liberation
Liberation flies flags of true freedom
Rules are constructed for order only

Giving it your all

Rise and rumble and give it your all
Great things will happen en masse
Quicken your steps going forward
Charge to a great table of action now
When your name is chosen you leave
Travel to great appointments in life

We have been given a great challenge
Our destiny to be one of two services
Either we enter the bell weather now
Or we hold on to several yesterdays
One service requires ultimate focus
Waiting can become a real death blow

Great people march out of obscurity
Shine where Rampant chaos reigns
Bring order to Wild rising confusion
Ones destiny remains as flag bearers
Raise the flag of peace and serenity
One contain rancor and confrontation

We may arise as One sane sentinel
Join a march of several sousaphones
Precise measurements is prerequisite
Our journey has evolved to protect
Protect the banners of the Heavens
Wave One are invisible life protectors

Several thousand Sentinels march
Marching across the open skyline
We have arisen to the majestic music
A Second mass service left yesterday
Two service arrives to become recoup
All bridges are rebuilt to Eden Flow

Charging yet into the bold brokenness
The second wave starts the healing
Leaders of Wild Rampant are quelled
Our mission has closed Chaos dam
One and Two service armies solidify
Amalgamation without Confrontation

USED PARTS OF TOOL BOXES

Question the pieces you have inherited
Unraveling in life leads to a real toolbox
Parts of life's brokeness may be fixed
We realize tools are available so we work
Prior tool men repaired mass brokeness
Now we are awarded the tools to fix all
Studying we understand all tool purposes
We become Tool Box Action Team Nine
There are nine broken structures ahead
Now we are the Action team repairing
Rebuild life with your second hand tools

Enlightenment

Signals flash in the cradle of my mind
This allows images to form as a vision
Significant events occur: open reminders
An evolution occurs to frame a Future
How will I anticipate the unraveling of it
I observe static I am in a frozen state now
I am totally incapable of any positive act
Time is suspended I see main crossroads
At the tri-juncture I choose Clarity Ave
I pass Luminous Way and Starla Street
Traveling swiftly I seek only finite truth
I must test everything to become a light
Enlightenment arrives as I am enmeshed
I seek my version of a Pontius Pilate truth
Enlightenment unfolds a personal picture
We are captive of our own idiosyncrasies

Arriving on Bleak Paths of Winter

When A group left Holland time was now
In time for the Autumnal Equinox winds
It begins a season of rough Atlantic seas
Winds will swell a sea and not give way
There are few placid days to this voyage
Gray Atlantic seas prevail in a wild flurry

Pilgrims pride and persistence carried all
They would not deter in any free pursuit
The Plymouth Company was determined
While they are sponsored they were free
No longer did they bow to anyone here
They only bowed to their Divine God

Their survival became an issue for other
Squanto a Pawtucket Indian aided them
On this first bleak winter barely survived
Stores of native fish then animals helped
Yet the life of a colony was special unity
Unity and peace became critical element

In a bleak path of a cold winter half died
Leadership is essential for good structure
They had written a Compact for living
Their Mayflower Compact was essential
It was not a mere bland treatise written
This is their roadmap for essential order

Riding through the bowels of hard winter
In the harsh climate they claimed strength
A mindset for survival was their support
Great men and woman rose as reliance
Plymouth ceded as a unitary authority
After many winters arose new Mass Bay

After one half dozen winters a success
Compacts and charters rule the colony
Yet through their free pursuit were saved
Saved by faith desire and real freedom

Spring Springs in January

Awake and observe the rush of Spring arriving in the Sonoran Desert as it quickly erases any thought of Winter
Moving across the landscape here and there new life is beginning to sprout in the dry and obscure rocky places
January is the month where a great desert song announces the miracle of new life arriving in the sparse fullness
will open my eyes to the desert flowers that surge and the desert birds that cello their arrival from Arrivipai
Here I will await the promise of refreshing spring rain that will bud and perfume the bland desert with hope

Pulsars wave through Deep Space

My great Galaxy Hunter Astroship Hexus climbs across liquid space searching vigorously for the defined Pulsars ahead
Journeying through the caverns of deep space we are aloft on a mission to identify the locations of massive Pulsar nodes
Amassing through several galaxies in space we discover a mysterious mass in Alpha Swirl galaxy a massive neutron star
Identification of this Pulsar is our task now and the Huge funnel of electromagnetic power surging at hyper speed now
This Pulsar is a fundamental wind spout in time space and traveling near must be with extreme caution and calibration
We signal to Station BEX that Pulsar B 1943 + 12 has magnetic pull of gravity five million times more power pull known
This Pulsar aptly named Super Suction Center has been measured and categorized as power effecting Alpha Swirl Galaxy
We are statistically determining its rotations its electromagnetic emissions and gravitational pull for space safety locks
Soon we break our map locators and once again power our protean fuel buds to exit and move across to distant galaxies

Charging Across the Massive Universes

We become the ready galaxy hunters spreading across the sky map of multiple universes that fill the void of Forever
Our immediate progress will appoint us the universe map builders that patrol the immense caverns of deep outer space
Mission 3723 requires us to track and establish the moving lines of galaxy changes and tracing universe precision patterns
We are ardent space presenters and pioneers who communicate with Space Survival Station Bex who map the unknown
Unimaginable constellations exist defying the known laws of controlled physics and astronomy we now do explore them
Magnificent mission 3723 will be the seventh of multiple voyages into deep space using renewable protean fuel buds
We are the Characteristic galaxy hunters plodding across the Universe of Luminescence searching for unknown life forms
While there exists relevant and formidable risks we are programmed to accept all difficulties and significant hardships
Discovery of several new premises, constellation systems and safe movable trail routes transcends all known catastrophe
Beginning outward from Station Bex we have chartered 3 known universes that populate the 4th millennium of Astrotime
Finding the path to brilliant universes beyond our brains imagination remains the massive challenge in the Forever void
The more that we discover the smaller our intelligence expansion becomes until it will reach a dwindling percentile now
We will adventure into the persistent patterns of Forever until we as a race expire or become Masters of the Forever Void.

Pivotal Statements

Where are the words that take me forward to my future destinations where I have hope to meet my expectations
Where are the great ideas that populate my vision on the video explosions that occupy massive spaces of time
Where are the people that are willing to guide me forward with all the appropriate questions and answers now
have located their agendas to follow but they all contain the legal caution words for my immediate destruction

Finding the path that leads to Truth

Live amongst the massive house structures built to satisfy the needs of the masses of resilient existing land populations
Thinking out loud I live in a block house segmented for the needs of people 40 years ago and they did not understand it
Mazes of rooms were built to accommodate the masses of populations privileged and promised yet real happiness faded
Houses do not build happiness since we segment our problems similar to the rooms we live in and never discover joy
Finding our true path requires significant time to explore and study; since the path to truth is not in the structure we live in
Truth resides in the soul of mans need and man has to extend his soul to assist others who do weep, mourn and bleed
Finding a sure path to truth requires a map, a trail and a plan to discover the continuous needs of mankind in a vale ahead
Create your path toward serenity and truth in the Shepard fields of Floribunda that bloom everlasting on the Emmaus road

Hollyhocks do Stand Tall

Paint lots of faded pink
Climbing they wave us
Wave for multitudes
In the early morning
Early morning is hope
We have lived one day
Turn around and see the activities of yesterday grind
Observation leads us to believe yesterday is powerless
Today we have control over a few things and then
Then revisit the faded pink hollyhocks and stand tall

Arriving At the Zenith

Finding the destination of choice I run to establish a claim
I will declare the Zenith of my existence as a promontory
Knowingly I cannot go any further the trail has now ended
Standing at this pinnacle I witness the madness I see below
Emotion and drive keeps civilization going at sonic speeds
The zenith that I witness evolves to a shocking view of all
Catapulting forward I see a raw view of man's inhumanity
I fall onto my knees to begin appeals to my highest power
The illogic of logic happening in a Vile valley of violence
Extricate remaining living and relocate them to Peacedale
Hours of anger and great turbulence crossed my pathways
Now I must attempt to heal the broken bodies of Beirut
Further I must consolidate the promises of New Peacedale
Tomorrow I go forward and Pray in Tongues for the many

Cutter Bee havior

Buzz of the busy bee often baffles me
Why make noise since I can also see
Smell of Mountain laurel grape sweet
I am drawn here where we both meet
I see your industrious pollen buzzing
Great noise hits my ear like awuzzing

Fly with the precision of a helicopter
Buzzing each blossom as pollen opter
Locate sweet nectars of satisfaction
Bring to the hive the sweet attraction
Success is the masses of new nymph
Crawl in Spring like airborne shrimp

Cutter bees are similar to you and me
Their busyness resembles a new tree
Growing so fast all must be attended
New generations constantly amended
Ready are forces of a pale new spring
Bring pollinator bee havior bustling

Mass of Ranunculus

I so quickly seized my old binoculars
To focus my eyes bursting ranunculus
These brilliant petal layers give a rise
It becomes a transfusion so petal wise
Electric pink a red recharge is my joy
I am reliving the magic of a little boy

Shades form cadence that colors song
Unique notes to reign so stem strong
All colors amass a beauty proceeding
I am an observer of interlocking Eden
Creation paints an image on my soul
Massive image that makes me whole

Observe the color and musical maze
See flowers open in a random blaze
Impromptu looks will speak a story
Rising in masses they wave in glory
Yes these are flowers that may deliver
A spring song that makes me quiver

I am now in tune with color in spring
Masses of Ranunculus make me sing

Bridging Our Lives

On one side of life I see newness
Crossing the great bridge I reflect
One side may remain as past glory
An other side of life can be hell like
Or this other side may grow paradise

It unfolds as I walk across a passage
Knowing I have no control I submit
Bridges in life bring me conclusions
Bridges in life allow me to unfold all
Bridges in life begin my departure

Have I understood my purposes yet
Entering the next bridge is a decision
Take myself serious and plan ahead
Roles in life can pull me down fast
Roles in life raise my spirit to height

Standing on an upward span I wonder
What can I really change on forward
I may change my attitudes and vision
I may amend my prejudice and fear
I may see people and places uniquely

Bridge my life to open passageways

Seeking a New Promise - Edward

We meander through life until we seek a New Promise for a future vision of precisely who we are
Profound change must occur for individuals to totally revamp self which exists - -Change is becoming
We must radically shuffle the deck of cards we were given to seek a massive new revision of our life
We will then become the abundant diversification of the new Edward that has washed himself clean
How this transformation will take place requires the dedication of the masses to approve and accept
The new promise is an uncovering of an alter other that emerges in the Midnight lights of Utopia

Clearly

While I see a mile ahead in the dense fog mask there is deep concern
Many others plod ahead without considering all the exceptional risks
It is my understanding that acute perception is not a multi-shared gift
I see what many other minds fail to comprehend and swiftly decipher
Motion and figuration is a guide to envision the real road at a distance
A slow deliberate speed is my pathway regulator against this adversity
Fog is cut through and immediately alarmed by the sound of noises
Hence I must have the windows of my ears attuned to active sounds
Forward I must have my vision field - open at a full panorama for safety
Clearly I have seen and heard a penetrating force for undefined adversity

Architectural Enhancements

I observe the massive rise and creative energy that aligns and configures
Genius desires to create the superstructures of tomorrow on todays map
Genius carries the genes of revision that revise and transform the cities
Clearly I foresee a link of great inspiration that connects to community
Designers often paint mental pictures on a horizon of endless potential
Then applying possibility thinking they envision the vista of tomorrow
All superstructures manifest an imprint of a single architects imagination
Buildings sometimes marry into the clouds while I lose my breathe now
Synthesize all simple lines with a significant space matter time concept
I will transform the world into a wonder of massive designs to consider

Allegiance

My allegiance is being and I rise from my bench and complete worship
My allegiance arises on American soil that which is constantly at a boil
Newness and naiveness contribute to my deep sense of patriotic fairness
Whatever and whenever I see wrong I constantly try to amend an issue
Where is the prime allegiance ascending from that rails to my own soul
I may search the open plains and prairies to locate perfect justification
Allegiance will enter my heart that boomerangs me back to a start point
At a start I read a document that all men were created equal:a beginning
My allegiance is to wisdom that collided with logic in a querulous mind
My allegiance is a family that every secular sycophant wants destroyed
My allegiance is to a New Jerusalem that I am searching for fastidiously

Flying Horses

Hold on to the reins now
The bell will ring soon
A magical tune will play
Horses will gallop here
Staying in our carousal
Round and round we go
Passing a prancing pole
Our calliope ride begins
We are on merry go round
having the ride of a life
We are on a venture to a great kingdom of surprise and joy
We are being driven on the wheel of glorious fascination
Our youth begins in a circle and then spreads and grows
Soon we conjoin larger.....elliptical in the circle of life

Riding the road through Northern California

A countryside is magnified in tall redwoods growing in tandem
They spur out of root systems and survive in the damp woods
Tall pillars arise surrounded by ferns and exotic moss growths
Redwoods are contained in a enchanted forest of wet foglands
How they sustain themselves in the primeval environs is magic
Living on the constant decaying matter they persist in the ideal
The mystical smell of the redwood stands provide environments
These environments provide a map of fresh air to new adventure
Rising smells of redorangebrown fill the cavities of my brain yet
Yet wet fog allows me to enjoy the aura of an instant tomorrow
A matrix of massive moss makes me mourn for open sky shining
I cannot feel safe in a haunted blankness with no other humans
Tear open a hole to the sky that I may clearly seek a blue horizo

Sentimental Journey

My many uncles served in World War II
Their valor and bravery were outstanding
My Uncle Joe never returned to Boston
Now only one uncle remains at home
The uncles never wanted to talk about it
Blazing movies communicate a story
The real stories stayed in the trenches

Young men got their eyes off of the war
Creating images of home to keep going
Pleasant Street USA emblazed thoughts
Home cooking kitchen smell remembered
Then small pleasures would give laughter
Games,mail,toys raises everyones morale
Now we will keep freedom flames alive

The children of the warriors were stoic
Proud their mother or father served us
Over many years the wear of war shows
Yet those who served all quiet contained
Observe glories of war - plastered screens
As memories etched an indelible picture
A legend of war became a cinema image

And heres to you Miss Betty Grable now
A Sentimental Journey is passing us by

Real Remembrance

We are together after tomorrow forever
A gathering of friends come to celebrate
One grand meal that will appeal to all

A gathering crowd is raised in special joy
All present are members of the wedding
Gathering welcome pieces are occurring

We are all rising to be gregariously happy
Our hosts and main party rise in oneness
It is a time of merging into remembrance

Locate the wonderment of one mindset
An occasion of togetherness and party It
is just for today we get to celebrate

Our mood is peaceful joyful and gentle
As members of a party we are real loving
For this party is contained toasting all

Brides and grooms to come will prepare
They have rehearsed the special words
Find all the great sentences to remember

We are being real here tonight as forever

Claim Transcendence

Brides bouquets are creatively special
Masses of mint roses twine together
They are regally arranged so perfect
Far above they are truly transcendent
A Memory of a special given day too
Stand back and observe bright white
The luminescence abounds all around
Special days come once in a lifetime
Allow the brilliance to penetrate you
See how aglow we are and transfixed
Observe the position of flowers here
Festive occasions hold flowers high
It is the beauty: is an aroma: is a flair

Bouquets are known for a short time
Whole wedding trains become fused
Amass of petals can trail life's journey
Use a flower wisely moving forward
The perfume of the wedding is blend
A blend lasts a few pebbles of to time
To time gives us a huge stake in life
There is to time to breathe and exhale
There is to time to raise your children
There is to time to take care of elders
There is to time to our own mortality

Rambling Thoughts

Success rolls to those seeking it
Most of us rise to states of shock
Living in suspended animation all
We fail to look ahead to envision
Our momentary existence is life
How we react to change is wonder
Often our movement is so limited
We cannot climb out of a cocoon
Locked in a cocoon we are frozen
Time limits say we will be crushed
A surrounding web case choking
Hiding from the future is not ours
We must break open our cocoon
Then we will be ready to glide
Gliding will lead to flying first
Then we will perfect a flight path
Once we are airborne a future is
It begins as we commence life
Patterns of possibility realized to
Realization maps a creative being
Treasured a mind moving forward
We cannot be still and exist long
Pour out your continual plans now
We are about several new options

Elm Avenue

remember its stately appearance
The massive spring flower beds
Only the wealthy and famous live
They live in a transition zone here
Younger wealth is moving south
Prestigious towns are further away
This parade of wealth on the move
Further travel on the Boston route
The masses are massing as buffalo
Herd mentality drives the leads
soon the great migration is done
may fence my wealth in purely
may guard my new castle close
may have a great retinue of glue
may attach myself to vital people
may become literally famous
may be safe but never satisfied

Wanda is Wandering

Enter a dialogue of repetition now
A magical marvelous mystic trail
It occurs and I follow its path yet
I need to know how perilous I am
My path may be rocky and jagged
Tomorrow I retest this pathway
Wanda is leading and pleading
All stops are measured and mined
This tour I am on is wandering
Whenever I see daylight I stop
Tomorrow I get off this tour bus
Tomorrow I will not be wandering
Tomorrow I likely am wondering
Where will Wanda wander to now

Universal Launch tracks Beckon

As we observe life's time capsule
Constantly see space bombarded
I have witnessed the drive onward
Space trajectory is now possible
Seek an upward climb as standard
There will be bus routes in space
Safety valves will reign in a climb
Protecting earthlings tantamount
Find the weekly schedule lurking
You have been called to alternates
Not all lines are operating weekly
Find the best path now to dwell on
Arise Space Buzz Ave is universal
We are mining paths of discovery
Open your launch window moving
We are a predecesor for uno moon
See the routes of discovery form
The lines of luminous are calling
Ready your brain waves for zoom
I seek the possible upward climb

End Conclusion

Recognize there is a final curtain
In the madness of culture its blank
No one recognizes an ending act
All participant expect full rides
When the cliff collapses CHAOS

Find your Joy Again

Allow the dust of the world to fall
I have accumulated shares of dust
If I am to transition I must change
Revise all the previous thoughts
Give way to the destructive habits
Let go of all malice and mischief
Realign the nebulous negativity
Allow the grudges to do a free fall

New pathways are drawn up today
I must follow this to a narrow gate
Revival trees are flowing in place
Majestic Orchids are carved life
Quiet streets listen in earnest now
Great swoon songs will be playing
Listen to echoes rising in oneness
Joy is a note of rising wonderment

Find all missed pieces of your soul
Work to realign to rejoin all pieces
Once your brokeness is recharged
A higher power can bring a tempo
A real tempo of resurgent inert joy
Yes there is joy in natures cadence
Rise up in newness you are alive
Resurgence of joy overwhelms us

Yes there is Joy permeating here
It is flowing as a river of life here
Capture the message ringing all
A mass of bliss is arising in all
Joy moves as a quick running rill
This experience patiently grows
So peace reverberates in the land
Joy, Joy, Joy bellows in greatness

Locate joy on this landscape here
Be charged to find all connections
Systematically be enjoined to all
Great feelings chime in your soul
The pace of hope and help arise
I am becoming a true chosen one
I am a pioneer of Joy abound now
Let no one steal my reverberation

Our Claim

How we grow to believe
Believe in our superiority
Then someone else claims
Someone will claim first
How we vent being second
Yet enjoy one to a moment
We must expand our vision field to a new vista ahead
Discover a new vision of prolong productive promise
Your mission in life is discover to uncover new gems
Radical race of technocratic tension grows to expand
Expanding magnitudes create massive new tech flex

We observe the time window of change mass anew
Our society is raging at out of speed dimensions now
Importance of being number one replaced by many
Our cultured society moves at a breakneck velocity
We are the pawns of the galloping research moving
In our time we will become obsolete octagons away
Our many sides will require at least eight fast fixes
Then many short updates will follow to keep us anew
If we allow ourselves to drift we will become Tikis
Our stone face will mirror our obsolete mind frozen
Yes we will be frozen in a distant time zone as Icons
We can claim abundant change only with wired brains

Calling A Great Pace

Pulsating quickly I observe time
Seeing the massive stretch of all
Masses of humanity are moving
Moving into the race of life now
Pace yourself to learn new skills
Pace the pathway ahead in speed
Moving pick up the pace gently
Be assured of your profound legs
Carry yourself to the break bridge
Find the stamina to arrive soon
Crowds are waving a gold crest
You are the first ten to cross over
Crossing you round the columns
Several columns arise as points
All structure points message gold
The worth of a race is compassion
Translate your gold into a be goal
Be a person of service climbing all
Find a career as service for others
Worthwhile life is meant to serve

Competition

Calmly we are told we are in a race
No instantaneous alarm is whistled
No athletic group shows to compete
What race is to flag my concern now
Where is the race going to take place
All real stadiums are empty dust lots
Yet the driving competition is coming
See the tire tracks of progress move
Allow all world engines moving space
You are in the global bubble changing
You are in the express lane blaring
React to a moving culture wave crest
Crest waves are arching fast furiously
Golden trumpets announce revision
Get on a rise and be a sure survivor
Otherwise you will be in a crest run
You will succumb in a drowning run
Yes there is a waging raging compete
A world compete will meet in toledo
Be ready toledo or accept a torpedo
A world culture is brewing anewing

Rise to the head of the wave to rave

Wall at Pronto Creek

Hit the wall at Pronto Creek hard
The native red stone allows a rise
We must arise to paint the picture
The massive stone reads a history
Pima and Papago's found water
Life was possible so near Sonora
Catapulting streams burst through
Bursting through the desert floor
Rumble now at an appointed time
The sustenance of life sustains us
We are given a satisfying drink
Life pours out a constant measure
It is our challenge to find passage
We are sojourners in the hot desert
It is part of our journey to connect
Connect the pieces necessary now
Our survival requires great vision
We need spiritual guidance ahead
Existence rolls to the water of life

64

Springs Delivery

How purposeful are these early flowers that generate a rebirth promise
Do we comprehend their great floral power that may open our thinking
It is unlikely we stop and consider their message on our life's journey
The early heralds of spring blast their trumpet sounds in all directions
Narcissus are an effective source of revelation to us as we finally age
Messages about rejuvenation make a sound that gives a deep meaning
Closely observe just how they are placed in nature so a word is passed
Sounding of their horns will play a melodious sound announcing JOY
Understand that your passing is a triumph of all your accomplishment
Arise to the uplift sound of your final rebirth in the everlasting chorus
Your arrival was expected and we prepared a place for your new voice

Press on to Recovery

Believing that life sometimes slides to the right of our reigning possibilities we constantly fight to get back to the center
To   be   insightful   often   we   cannot   translate
why   and   how   this   happens

Perhaps it means that we just have not fully recovered   from our tragic event

Running on Zuni Time

There is a cultural gap that never meets at the Avenue of Profound Yesterdays since our folkways are learned
Although we understand this we never fill the gap so often we try with our simplicity to understand at base level
Time equates to accomplishment in some cultures in other cultures time is a point on the horizon coming soon
Tomorrow may be Tuesday and I will meet you on Tuesday sometime in the Tuesdays of tomorrows tomorrow

As the River Flows Forward

tremendous flow of waters rush from the mountains surrounding the rivers of commerce and grand contentment in the far west
Rushing forward all rills have carved themselves and join excited brooks that join streams and pass rippling to some small tributaries
Then the tributaries rage onward to join the rivers that sustain the masses of human existence here
How the roaring water passes so vibrantly across our vision field showing its force and power now
As the season of Spring passes before us see how the raging waters slow as snow melt will recede
Then the storms of late summer will perk up the maddening flows and serve as a active reminder
As a river flows forward our lives are passing with it sometimes moving rapidly then to a slow crawl
What then.........the river marks the progression and recession of our life's journey forward in time
We must retain our courage so we may intercede carefully with our human issues as we flow along
Sometimes we must move at lightening speed then other times we will require slow tedious action
The river flow characterized the motion that we must proceed at to handle life's massive challenges
Our human patience is tested by a great river of life that we pass through and so often changes flow

Coming to grips with a new reality : Progress

Patterns of days change and revise in their character while they evolve over the horizon and revolve in specific uniqueness
Monday had its own history, weather pattern, birth number, death number, promotion, unique events and joyful times until
of course Tuesday arose and found itself in a parade of listless statistics, problematic demographics and undefined wines
When Wednesday to Sunday must retreat and think how they must compete to run on their feet with a new reality :Progress

At My Doorstep

In the alcove at my front door is a small bench to crash on in an emergency and to allow for a short rest awhile
Yet no one has taken up residency here except for a pair of Mockingbirds who hover above in my rubber plant
Birds must be building a nest to raise a brood above a majestic small bench reserved for future unknown guests
Someday I expect that a preacher will come and preach or a marketing mouthpiece will promote a goat or boat
Then at other times an official will have me sign to receive wine or a candidate will come along to help educate
At my doorstep all I want is my children to sit and ring a bell to let me know all is swell and we can stay awhile

Dressed in Purple Aroma

There is a certain shade of Purple that captivates your mind in time gaze
You become lazed in a haze of a deep lilac vase that generates an aroma
Finding an upright beauty blaze will allow you to enter a proto phase
Follow your mindset to a craze that moves you far from a lavender gaze
Now you may laze on pillow top maze allowing you to sing violet praise
You may rise and raise a candle in praise of violet violas playing a craze
Color your days in a simple phrase that allows royal tyrian cloth to blaze
Find your purpose to become chaise then allow others to find glad ways
Life is dressed in a Purple aroma of rays planning how to taze your ways
Arise from a daze in a majestic lavender mindset and rephrase the future

March of the Corner Cuts

In streams of my dreams I envision hands of my bands cutting corners
Rolls of drums strum and play for the alums who throw them crumbs
Cutting corners will bring mourners who get excited listening to scorners
I need to correct the line and keep it fine to call it mine and give it spine
Marching bands across the lands requires stands to maintain the brands
My job with guts will eliminate buts to get out of the ruts to begin struts
This band will look sharp as I remove the tarp to the strings of a Harp
Yes I will put on pageantry and give it a day to spray and begin a foray
Pay attention to the mention of my new invention we move in pretension
Finally my decision improves precision and recision using our provision
Who cuts corners are goners reserved for my significant serious mourners
Who will bury the clandestine foreigners who dares to critique performers

Express Truck

We are expecting a special Be livery by the young man in charge of delivery
Deegan will get it done in the morning sun and have a lot of fun doing the run
Yes we are getting it done backing it up and dumping the yard trash by the ton
We have not seen a yard so clean since a lean garbage machine cut the beans
This truck is on a roll to go catch a tadpole or remember a knoll where to troll
The young man in charge will put refuge on a barge near my old ancient garage
He knows with a little luck how to get a sleek black truck to pick up the muck
This young man has taken command of a little black truck to meet the demand
Yes there is a run promptly now that may stun those who shun a curve that spun
Delivery is our goal we plan to stay whole for every living soul getting a bowl
Express to get there without distress and not depress all that needs to do reassess
We are depending on vending so fill all machines with jelly beans especially greens

IRIS MORNING

As the shadow Gives Umbra

It has become the garden delight
Shadows race across from night
Yes it becomes a beauty in a light
Right winds provide petals might
Great firm stems hold it upright The beauty of the
morning illustrates a floral flight Patterns of promise
draping over pleasing to alight   I await a butterfly
to land on the premises so tight Find a camera to
capture an image of a magic sight Time will

manipulate a drawing of massive plight   I can only
still nature for a few moments
this bright

As the Morning Dew Settles

There is a statement that is made As the morning
flowers glimmer Great swaths of petals shimmer
Early sun paints a different hue Perhaps it occurs
from early dew A blending between shadows and a
bird that flew   Maybe it was contained in strong
winds that blew There is a certain slant of sun light

Paths of Inland Rivers

Inland rivers pour into
origins where creation
begins
Waters will lead you into
a wellspring of cascading
hope
Inland rivers pour forth as
an eternal rushing rumble
Inland rivers are now alive
Inland rivers are vibrant and charging with the essentials of life
Inland rivers are brimming and teeming with potential promise
Inland rivers are rising and raging with powerful unbound forces
Inland rivers are totally overflowing with remnants of good life

Inland rivers are running with a real massive powerful impetus
Inland rivers drive themselves exuberantly to the source of life

Oh I have seen inland rivers that are roaring with driving energy
Oh I have seen the spillways that bound forth in magnificence
Oh I open my eyes to future flows and to future flows beyond

Oh inland rivers you brought me to the Eden of my existence

Rising on the San Juan Isle Ferry boat

Who would have ever thought Mary would traverse at sea
Crossing Sqagit Bay we were ripped with a real sea squall
While we stayed afloat we were driven far off our course
Patrons worried about connections we held our stomachs

Words That Penetrate

Listening is an active tool in life
When they gather to meet... listen
Words cannot change your vision
Words can enhance your direction
Sometimes the sacred word sparks
Follow a spark that gives you life
What you heard in the chapel rang
The bell words became new action
You are driven by good directions
While impulses are often neutral
Find an anointed pathway forward
Great ideas are spiritual dynamite
Blasting forward is true challenge
Do not look backward... sizzle on
Life is a long and narrow roadway
Prepare now for all future bumps
The initial direction we received
This was a prime ingredient for us
Everything added was pure faith
Did you use words that penetrate

Precariously

Climbing the stairs at Coit Tower
Must be executed cautiously now
The wear of time to footprints are
Grinding all stones:human erosion
Our walk up can be a real classic
Hang onto a rail so you never fail
We are fearless climbers to the top
Arriving at a top takes momentum
Our energy levels are momentous
We are not slowed by all adversity
We are challenged on on upward
Arrival at tiptop can be precarious
Find the eloquent words 'hang on'
We are but mortals being lifted up
Our view of the bay is fascination
Where lifes view are unobstructed
We must see the whole foundation
Knowing all the precarious spots
We will navigate on this mountain
We will chart a precarious course

South Mountain Park

A desert will fan its stored up beauty
Desert plants paint colors landscapes
Often opening to a redyelloworange
In the wand of harsh heat I am beat
Still the mountainside flourishes here
During spring see poppies to lupines
Announce Saguaros and Palo Verde
Then Paint Brush and Moon Flowers
Find Desert Daisies and blue Agave
A segmented flowering in adobe clay
A Sonoran Desert raises new Ocotille
Small Palo Verde burst with Yellow
Then later the Ironwood rays purple
Seasons in a desert wait for monsoon
Lightning bolts emphatically slams
A desert down pour is a summer call
Summer calls a just ready thirstiness
Arise from the mountain to arroyos
A short summer respite gives life no
After the massive storm a cooling of
Then the smell of creosote to ozone
Storms pass through as a benediction
An anointed odor of Sonoran change

Riding the Horse to a Quick Gallop

Across the open plains of Missouri I ride the Arabian horse of my dreams to a mission of real great importance
Riding at breakneck speed I am racing to get to the far end of Joplin before the curtain of sunset draws closed
My great mission to inform the people that a mass of locusts are raging across the Great Plains soon to arrive
All who are available to man poison jet pumpers need to be in position by daybreak as locusts hordes congeal
From a long distance we can hear the insect cloud buzz hum while the number of pumpers are ready to blast
Then out of the wind breaker tree line come brigades of locust marauders flying.... so our cannon pumpers fire
Thousands of vagrant locust crash all over.. diminishing a frontal attack.. cannons prime blasts save cornfields

uxtaposition

Losing a game is not very amusing yet may be a start of self recognition
We may play hard in competition but our real game is out of commission
We believe we are so greatly talented yet competition writes a definition
Our smart foe is challenging us but our idyllic game is in decomposition
So we will continue to allow them to see our image a specific admission
Time has caught up so our game needs adjusting from a sport technician
Running full steam ahead can be an exceptionally rigorous proposition
Locate the spire and bring on the fire we have begun our juxtaposition

My Mind is a Blank

At various times our focus becomes unfocused and conceptually blurry
Under the microscope of life we wander and forget our set of objectives
On a day we are to be interviewed for an important assignment we blank
Our whole thought process becomes a shallow pool of end statements
Reviewing our oral presentation we fail to connect the dots of direction
Confirmation of our weakness rises before us bellowing:we lack purpose
New mission opens to call us to action: Remain alert in all circumstances
Time flashes by us in rapid order so..... my mind is a blank can wear thin
Active preparation and thorough research imbue us with powerful words
Tomorrow our time is in line going forward... Our campaign commenced

Restoration

In our brokeness we struggle to become whole again... strive to oneness
It is in our personhood that we rebel to uniqueness then define its failure
How we pick up all the shattered pieces will become our great mission
At times pieces become immovable we cannot break out of the old life
Old bonds are difficult to break and be set free from lodged in quicksand
Thinking ahead we need to envision our future singularity and freedom
Old dungeons reek of yesterdays death and destruction can carry an odor
Restoration must proceed to resuscitate us to our renewed oneself intact
We say arise once again so our priorities renew as we repair soul damage
Finally we become whole: restoration will breathe new life and ambition

Seeing A Mass Arising

Beyond my first horizon a Bellow
Then a more thunderous resound
A great shaking and ground moves
Tone trumpets above blare victory
An in-comprehensive action occur
Great prophet of Wisdom is gone
Great Prophet of healing has left
Great Teacher of all has left school
Great Words remain to guide us all
Now we patiently await a next act
I will arise in the world wind now
I will be changed in mass revision
I am here now instructed to relate

We are all in a boat time traveling
Each of us will have departures
Each of us will have new arrivals
Once all disfunction's are aboard
Then a mass rebellion takes place
The boat will be run by radicals
A Mass Arising will tolerate uno
Uno will speak for all then silence
Speak in the now or be silenced
Voices are streaming across miles
Networks speak we are inundated
Arise in new mornings and labor
Vineyards will speak to the vines
My life is entwined in the truth
Truth is hard to uncover in vines
Find truth in grapes of compassion

Locate your Soul

We follow various roads to sanity
Often sanity escapes us as we race
We race to acquire wealth or fame
Our soul is not at peace with these
Driven to find shade in the heat
The canopy of life provides light
Our soul seeks the forest canopy
Forest tree dominate a souls shade
Our soul seeks a credo of concern
We are shaped by worldly images
Soul seeks God's face out of chaos

Search for Happiness

My constant and tenuous search is
My search is to find a happiness
While I search for the Happy Road
Certainly I find Broken Boulevard

Pathways to positive thinking are
Positive thinking evolves to hope
Hope emanates as a smiling flag
Happiness is rippling in a breeze
The wind will drive happiness on
A gust of wind ripples happiness
Happiness bounces to prudence
Prudence way allows for testing
We test for our self centeredness
We test for our magnificent goal
We test for our friendship trail
We test for compassion to others
We test for repeat assisting needs
We test for hands across the water
We test for allowance for others
We pass the test with our soul
Soul delivers the happiness rate
Those in service find happiness

Constant Crystalline

Enamored by the colors of Pins
I see a remarkable design now
Here a bench man connects lines
Lines of Pearls match to emeralds
Forest Green emeralds spin here
Spinning as a wave across center
Behind the wave effect more turns
An end of waves ruby red stones
The pin designer shows tsunami
Without hope great Tsunami wave
Many lost in bench mans design
A Wall of design mirrors pictures
While a constant crystalline shines
Shine on bodies overcome now
Massive tsunamis cover our lives
Map a constant model to yourself
Pioneer the sapphire of precision
Seek a blue crystalline conclusion

Upon Seeing Dali's 'Corpus Hypercubicus'

Compassion is on the picture face
A woman driven by emotion now
Surrounded by sadness and fear
Her only son has passed upward
Cubes are more brutal than nails
Depicting a mass agony and pain
Aware of the sacrifice I see depth
There is mass concentration about
My senses are numb to its reality
While I see no blood I see victory
The whole human race can now g
Risen Chrism chosen for believers
Witness a great transformation
You are about passing through all
Yes pass through the waters to life
Resurrection .....A 2,000 year gift

Laminate

I will cover the mistakes and lamina
No one can see my error imperfectio
Hiding small scuffs and nicks is goo
Correcting a scratch or bend is mend
Restoring is a promise process given
We all desire the perfect piece alway
Work to illuminate out mistakes now
Attempt to elucidate and recreate all
Finding my core abilities I medicate
I now laminate so I get to propagate
My gifts are multitudinal to madness

eet At the Crossroads to Pass on the Message

Sometimes in lifes passage we are required to be silent when chaos arrives
Then we may be recruited to be a sentinel of truth passing the Mirror Code
Meet us at our crossroads and speak a clear concise code of embedded truth
Find the passageways on the road that meets up to the messengers of Mirar
They will find the trail to the Open Bellow and resound the treatise to all
Listen to the flow of right relationships and honest criticism rebound here
Our truth cannot be a hollow echo in hell but rather a bastion of betterment
Our truth cannot be a self-serving sequence that benefits just a few mortals
Our truth must be a passage to discovery that finds a path to sound judgement
Our truth must shine in the sunlight for all citizens to see and understand now
Massing on the borders of light are those who will charge to bring dark chaos
Find a correct button on Mirror Code: relay a beacon of powerful open arrays
We are at the cusp of change and it must be accomplished in grand unison
In our current continuum all factional closed door decisions bring decadence
ise and be informed: Power of the Great Republic aligns to four great freedom bells - truth, justice, wisdom and hope

Rococo

y life at times has been a series changing and rearranging to meet my expectations that surround my real rococo mindset
amining the steps I took I am surprised I survived the vision of my peers as everything was an elaborate ornamentation
y presentations were a thundercloud of asymmetrical formats massively designed to see the true power of great business
I my attempts to give a work we had accomplished a graceful pat on the back was attacked by just give us our facts Jack

Perceiving Our Imperfection

e often look at ourselves from many different angles and find bad habits that we eventually attempt to change
e often see our mirror image different than our compatriots so we revise ourselves to meet ourselves at a door
mass of catapulting criticism may arise and rumble driven by molten hot magma of hearsay and manipulation
ake your total physiognomy and maintain a code of silence your critics be many while your flaws be invisible

Finding Treasures Not Realized

Massing ahead I see the prizes I want : Desire drives me to achieve my goals
Somehow I gallop on lifes high plateau : yet I am lost in a morass of myself
Ambulating ahead I see it is about me : Perhaps it is coming to my crossroad
Seeking the treasures I sought.. empty : I will rise and soul search to take note
Locate a profound passage of change : Rearrange the priorities of lifes train
The turbo engine races at bullet speed :Knowingly I pass up the golden rose

As life will pass station after station : Realize the final stop is Salisbury Beach

Help is the Word of Wisdom that is difficult to Shout

How many times did we struggle in a dark moat unwilling to call help?
How did we emotionally grasp failure in our individual breakout cells?
How did we stand up after all our primary ideas were declared lacking
How was our disposition once we are declared to be massively obtuse?
Remember help is a shout - failure a temporary human condition-
and your ideas were there to help contribute to massive sweet serenity
arch to a continued vision that inspired your heart and never relinquish your underlying message of true wisdom flow
hen you detect that one out of a group of many needs adjustment then your role of prime wisdom mitigator will enter
st when the bell rings, the chimes resonate, and the buzz of life calls : become the word of wisdom to answer the shout

Seeking Best Outcomes

I desire to always respond in truth yet
Yet often there is a twist in the wind
Our humanity causes a shift in color
When I should have yelled teal blue
Instead I said medium sky blue hue
It is not in the color but final outcome

My role in life rides on preciseness
My role expects others to follow this
When I fail to come to common terms
When I fail to yield the best answer
Instead I peal away layers and judge
It is not in naming options but reality

When I need to hypothesize potential
I must assess the best I am capable of
When I observe the many end games
Locate the corner crevices of living
Peal away my emotional fear or loss
Move ahead of opinion get true value

Best outcome:a challenge to arrive at!

Our Grand Alliance

Alliances are temporary in springtime
Revolution in new life begins quickly
Masses crawl from the ground cradle
Other creatures arise from a cocoon
Chirpers find the sediment and sticks
Other animals find soft beds to birth
See a great abundance of pale green
A forest begins a mass genesis rebirth
Observe the countryside is flowering
You are in the recall morning of life
Ally yourself to a new grand alliance
Your metamorphosis now a beginning

The Fragile Finger Of Fate

Pointing at us is the finger of decision
At the point we are at we cannot stall
Action is a mystical call we now hear
Seeing there are no concise answers
Our thoughts must be in true oneness
Soul searching questions are required
What would Alex want us to think to
What would Alex see as real critical
What would Alex do for us similarly
Express our opinions in a open forum
Allow others to weigh all the issues
We need to come to rapid conclusions
All his children now are in agreement
Ensign Alex will be buried at sea now

Champion of the Beet Patch

Every year I have grown banner crops
Every Year I am giving bunches away
My back entry is beet red from harvest
A great abundance of beets always arise
Dark red beets find the soil delicious now

Yet this year it was a cold winter colder
Beets grew in abundance and real close
A crowded cavern crowded out masses
What the cold and crowd made to occur
My harvest was puny and pittaling here
I have lost my beet patch championship
So I will refeed my sad soil once again
So I will plant cautiously with distance
So I will converse to my expert gardeners
Next year I raise expectations and beets
Next year I may regain and win a Borche
Next year I may declare beets abounded

Possibilities

In our worst performance to date
We get a few claps but not accolades
Our best delivery act is stale bread
Thus change must mark our actions
Inevitably we revise old repertoires
Unsureness marks our real thoughts

Revision in a buzz mission in our life
We may get depressed in new roles
Often become lethargic or neutral
Finding ourselves is base new action
We are rolling like a deuce and a half
Find a brave driver and we roll in one

Our possibilities are raw wild assets
Tweak yourself and change a program
Marching forward there is a new goal
Arrange change to mark a rearrange
Possibilities are strange amidst Chaos
We now march in a solo man brand

Possibilities restructure life and limbs
Get in a sequence of change or falter

In Quest of the Morning

Rush of circumstances require brakes
When streams of extreme occur: Stop
Slow a bustle of morning :Sometimes
Remember: Remedial actions work
Clarify: What is chasing or erasing
See: Every morning is a rabbit run
Carefully plan your morning gallop
Tomorrow is the critical mass move
Execute each morning quest precisely

Golden Gate Bridge Suspension

Witness the whiplash wind winding here
Powerfully it waves a small trough ripple
Above the guardian towers hold together
The bay acts as a suction cup breathing
A whistling sound can be very ominous
Hold yourself to a certain level awareness
The fog beat of denseness is a bear trap
Rumbles in the earth crust is a warning
Suspended in suspended animation now
Observe the ridge from the Presidio here
Whenever there is a shake and tumble
Anchor yourself in quicksand and rope
Ride the suspense and fence the hillside
Hope for no hill slide and fissure cracks
We are Golden if we are still standing up
Rise be perked anew with gratefulness
You survived a 7.9 earthquake.... Breathe

A Lack of Lustre

The crowd searches for a personal glow
Most of us are lacking this magic lustre
Those who possess it have an arena entry
Most of the rest of us just move in a flow
Climbing a ladder of such grand persona
We find that few have an outward corona
Perhaps it is only our best friend Ramon
So we need to protect that girl of Verona
Our secular synchophants will destroy it
Driving fame to an edge of a ledge to fit
See a young woman as a manipulated w
Driven so vainly and causing her to split
Was there something said that caused a
Was it really lack of lustre falling in a p

Our Personal Lustre Observe

Lustre only lasts for a few short moment
Our time is on a scale and so very limite
Measure your short time on a stage of li
We do have one window to shine throug
Locate your best strategy to bask in glo
We are put here for a purpose and stretc
Be of good service and smile in sunshin
We all are forgotten in the beauty of tim
All they do remember:our humble servi
Work a special focused activity and smi
Your biography was written in
hieroglyphics

Lollygagging in La Mancha

Good man Don Quixote first hollers Fa
There is no lollygagging in La Mancha
There is a guard that leads you forward
He will slow progress down considerab
When a challenge is offered what move

Shade Cover

Arizona Sun Blisters your brain
Masses defer to a shady glade
In a midst of the heat: get relief
To umbras of the ashes I retreat
Hide under the Aspen branches
Make a retrench to a Ponderosa
Find ambience in the high Oaks
I am a seeker of High Umbrage
ikening a shade cover: I dash to keep a massive covered profile
Ay cool attitude of natural branches support my essential cover

PRALINES

Juts sugar and sometimes chocolate creme fill my test stocking
At other times it dances in my ice cream flavor as an alternative
omorrow I am having a praline birthday Watch I am drooling

Tantamount

Tantamount to success are some ingredients of a start up
company Laboring in a field of needs and wants are feisty new
customers What ideas can I create and deliver to the masses of
New Carabi Find the tickle point of market and build a structure
of base word Base word is a critical component of wonderment
and adoration Mass hysteria will hit the streets and the public
will swoon now My Rabadoodak game clothes and perfume: A
true new standout Tantamount was my entry on the static
Boulevard of Dreariness I have a rejuvenated marketplace for a
first time in twelve years Now they must give me a ticker tape
parade on Parabola Avenue I swung the door open twice and I
owe it my tantamount success I went through two doors
achieving my ongoing glowing success Remember the hard
work and the legions of people that assisted Tomorrow a

The Rocky Coast

ur land slopes at a steep angle to the sea
ulls surround our campfire on a hillside
hey glide with the rhythm of spring tide
ne thing that covers all : a lone pine tree
ynthesize nature now and her fog occurs
'e are here marooned in a camp ground
et the fires warm our hearts in our circle
/e are placidly enjoying the coastal fog
'e are hidden in natures own disguises
ere is enough vision to see the rocks
ligned we are visitors of a rocky coast
lultitudes of sea life wave us incognito
cky coast is home to tide pool species
ocks hide some sea creatures for safety
ocky coasts will preserve land mass life
oasts are Inter Zones for the multitudes
rise and observe natures magnitudes
'e have inherited a massive true jewel

Palisades

the distance are the steep lined cliffs
hey amaze me as all high walls of life
repare me as a cliff hangar holding on
fty cliffs challenge my total psyche

Rising Monoliths

Rock monoliths rise on the Pacific shelf
Along a Pacific highway I read meaning
Amassing along : short shelves anchor all
Monoliths carve a viable sea life habitant
Monoliths speak to the shortness of time
Staunchly formed by the wind and waves
they become the guardians of a coastline
Witness their purpose:they are protectors
Standing watch they hold a land together
Monoliths are the angels of the landscape
Monoliths serve as a first sea pummeling
If they disappear islands are now exposed
Jutting out on a coast rocks provide a net
Monoliths keep erosive forces in a check
Sea birds gather to mate and give us birth
Next generations perch and ascend rocks
Gulls to Terns keep a coast whistle clean
Coasting on the thermals is an outline sea
Waves engulf rock formations eroding all
Times window of power erase has begun
Bit by bit stone grains are broken blasted
A hollowing out occurs at a sea shoreline
Protective monoliths will then disappear
Continuing erosive power will soon arise
Land forms will gently slide into oceans
Ocean appetite can devour land formation
Await to see a coastal flooding continuing

Playing with Toys

Small children make toys their tiny world
Often their creative energies will explode
A duck takes flight in an inordinate way
An Interplanetary space ship zooms up
Beautiful dolls become real companions
Treasured games become a competition
Train engines find a trail without tracks
Nurse uniforms and bandaids are surreal
Comic book characters now become alive
Stuffed animals retain a special bed space
Many colored and shaped blocks are built
Coloring books and sticker books create
Plastic devices to make sports champions
Books help us learn those real fantasies
We are wowed with a multitude of toys
Mold your toys into your lifes ambition
Tomorrow you are a doctor or engineer
Fine tune all your toys into your dreams

Tepid

Tepid is an attitude I sometimes hold to
Understanding when things are in flux
Then when a fog lifts in the new horizon
Attitude must be dug in and justified now
Dig in and support your revised thinking!

Rising to Meet The Morning

See how you greet the new morning as it emerges over a horizon of great hope and great awakening
You have been conditioned to expect the sun to rise and a horizontal picture of familiarity unchanged
ARISE! the new morning is coming like a great cataclysm full of twisting change and massive rearrange
You are being rein formed that you will be reformed and revitalized on a great morning of departure
You will be transformed and rearranged so you flow through the trees and mountains as you rise now
Tomorrow is an hour of revision, you reach a decision you have been transformed as a renewed mind

Waimea Canyon

I walked to the edge of the cat walk pad and overlooked a canyon below
Great buttes and monoliths rise to shadow all deep winding crevice trails
Grass and small bushes spring out of the sides of red rock structures here
For miles light haze settles upon a canyon creation lending an eeriness
Over the high ridges the orangeredbrown rock and stone lay in dust piles
Dust piles are awaiting a thunderous thunderstorm to wash loose debris
Yet from my perspective the canyon lines and ruffles remain so natural
Here I see a magnificent remainder of two thousand volcanic eruptions
Tomorrow the buttes and monoliths may shake again in slow disturbance
Possible flows of lava may create a new lustre in times new continuum

The Door

I can open and close the door and I am ready to let you come inside here
First you need to know the magic words and be able to recite them fast
The words are simple and clear Please play games and puzzles with me
Set time to help me grow right now and little things are really helpful
I am in your kaleidoscope for a short time so you are my big helper now
All the small things you do will give an example of great beginnings so
So let us get started and challenge the days and weeks racing ahead here
I am at your full attention so let us follow this great companionship now
Plying ahead swiftly we will open several doors as I mature and you lea
Then I will grow up and I will enter doors that are in my future beyond

Kauai Lighthouse

A cruise liner closes in on the shoreline and Kauai Lighthouse appears
Mellow blue waters lap the shore and invite us to come and be visitors
Small craft boats buzz the waters below us and indicate our destination
Our berth will be waiting for us at a massive dockside pier with vendors
This pale white lighthouse juts out on a peninsula : a symbol of welcome
Since there are no Aloha natives we have been transformed by a symbol
A lighthouse as an inspiring symbol of hope and translucent redirection
Often when we are in significant need a lighthouse gives a guiding light
The light mirrors our need to map our way through the strong currents
Tomorrow a Tsunami may drive us off course.. continue to seek the light

Volcanic Beach Rising

Monstrous rocks and hardened lava flow surround a teal blue beach
I have arrived 700 years too late to observe several volcanic eruptions
The rolling waves beat on the beach and pummel the rock into pumice
Ages pass by and more eruptions litter the beach with magma flowing
Then a cooling off period creates a period of stability and new erosion
The carved inlet beach represents years of creation by a master creator
Shorelines are carved by molten lava that sizzles in the warm sunlight
Oceans salt waters steam in the lava heat slowly until it soon dissipates
Tides move and rise and fall and lend a piece of pumice to all sea life
Periods of quiet remain on inactive lava cones until anger reappears
Volcanic anger will recreate new statements about a rising inlet beach

Arriving on Time

t is my passion to be right on time exactly, precisely and concisely so I am all about getting started when the last second is departing
Watching the clock I observe exactly sixteen minutes of travel to unravel and appear at my destination looking like Captain Marbel
o I roll down the road and begin moving like a toad and do everything to lighten the load changing my modes with no one to goad
Racing with time I try to climb up atop of my prime squeezing a lime talking in mime with no one to rhyme : late due to road slime

How Self Centerness Destroys Us

No adequate manner will describe our individual behaviors as we move forward in an attempt to assist others
Mindset Open Door is a project utilized to assist those who are really down and out to whom we call brothers
Yet many walk a different direction and live in a massive separate field called 'Lack of any specific
compassion' Someday we observe 'what is all about me' is contained as a lonely rigid narrow solitary nursing
ome passion Silence may give rise to requiems for all those trapped in their own image until their ashes are
eleased in a sea Finding an appropriate place is critical for those remembered at certain acceptable destination

---

Rays on the Bay
Smooth Rolling Waves Cresting in the Cove

n ebb and flow enters the small inlet bay and provides a small shelter for the abundant Hawaiian sea creatures
Carved small lagoons provide the great Shore House of majestic unique creation
Great Shore Houses of amorphous seaweed and coral become the Pacific nurseries
Building upon the small retreats and coverings small sea life reside and subsist here
Marvels of the surrounding Ocean all sea life blends into the labyrinth of existence
Rippling tides provide the power wave of ocean movement that sustains sea masses
Waves move as ocean wind giving new homes for sea creatures displacing others
Coves remain as a home perhaps similar to the land creating then recreating again

Finding No Real Truth of the Matter

Weighing in for a dispute I observe how angry the masses become if they sense to any degree that they have been purposely slighted
pen forums are not always available to sort out poor treatment lack of concern unwillingness to pay a vendor and lesser altercations
sing storms of street anger drive people families and groups to state their case demanding fairness, equity, truth, and honest payment
nocent streets fields houses and businesses place a smashing jaw breaking accident settling no arguments, anger or confrontations

---

Like a Fish Out of Water Streaming

Fish can walk on a fence
Their plates are not dense
Their attitudes make sense
They sub in specific tense
They bunch to crawl hence
Nillyilly lilly find expense
The cost of a fish dancing on a fence is real immense
Broken pickets mashed uprights bent rods to whence
We need to smooth a transition so fish get confidence
Smile be positive moving slowly into a water trench
A fish out of water can be a real massive hindrance

See them swim in tubs swirl around splash and drench
Pilot our boat and allow the fish room on our bench
Give them a glass, celebrate fulfill their need quench
Their skin becomes hardened similar to a pipe wrench
Strolling along their scales transform to a total clench
Following a trail in the woods entitled a super trench
Wiggling and wobbling they dance similar to a wench
Rising once more they waltz across trails never flinch
Their eyes are affixed on moving toward a sea trench
Surrounding us are brown mud packs exuding stench
Moving hence can be a dense inch crawl to retrench

Windmill of Chime

Windmill of time capsulate clear sky
Winding into jet streams upside down
Dispatching fresh batches of oxygen
Inhale and exhale on this landscape
Flowing air streams in emphatic ways
Create energy, grind corn and breath
Windmill emissions are clean to clear
They rotate in a sky like Ursa the bear
Whirring motion creates a devotion to
The powerhouse pound sets a sound
Create notes for purring young kittens
Threshing fresh winds a musical time
Begin this rhyme of musical sublime
Creaking and whirring to luring notes
Winds glide and ride a low symphony
Certain chimes climb the wind scales
Scaling and drive in a grass harp field
Catching the driving gusts with notes
Notes remain without a shear doubt
Winding winds deliver end melody
Several end melodies create a song
Great songs of this windmill blend
Blending across the land creating joy
Joy flows as windmills turn out song
Windmills become a lifting landscape

Slide Rides begin

I now observe the slide ride ahead
Vroom is the road that I will trace
Charging upon the top there is joy
Challenge the great slippery road
I am readying my hands and feet
I see the bottom of the ending ride
Soft landings is a great terminus
Piles of sand loom at the bottom
My excitement is growing quickly
I decide where I will be traversing
Whether I hold on slowly to a side
I decide leave slow or blast ahead
It is my turn to slide so I am ready
A great thrill is about to begin now
I ply my hands to the slide rails
I see what is about to happen here
My mind is focused in the slide
Happy I am going down a slippery
My hands are raised in affirmation
This is great.. a fun run has begun

Oak Creek Side Trail

Running off the Kabaib plateau wate
Water worms its way into a channel
It gurgles down from the steeples
Red rock steeples permeate here
Window of a spiritual nature wea
Sandstone windows in red steeple
Along the quiet flow I am hidden
Maples and oaks rise to the skies
Blending the water path cleanses
Oak creek washes the redorange
It repaints the stream bed awash
Finding it beckoning I am on edg
The edge is a trickle of ice water
My numb feet understand origins
Origins run on San Francisco pea
Snow melt is christening my toes
Nature is teaching me new lesson
Frogs and fish relish cold waters
I must be in readiness for nature
Creek water refreshes and numbs

Fulfilling our Great Destiny

Waddling through the most difficult circumstances we slowly recover our quiet composure to smile
A great driving wind will blow incessantly to slow our progress through our lifes most brutal storms
Often we are left remaining to suffer and recover our best on our own that speaks loudly for courage
Initially our total bounce back and sure fire recovery leans heavily upon our ability to cope with facts
We are alone on this planet and our resolve to be a survivor hinges upon our total dynamic attitude
Allow wisdom from above to permeate our mindset and chunk through rough spots with resonance

Sailing on Quincy Bay

I remember a colleague named Bob who lived to sail across the waters
Often on occasion we would set sail from the Squantum Yaught at Five
For two or three hours we would navigate across to Hog or Peddocks
Without a plan or purpose the Thunderbird would angle in the wind now
How I would see the sea as mate and sailor in charge of having orders
Clearly my orders were to find the sea wind and set sail for destinations
In my youth I found a friend who would allow me to avoid the buoys
He instructed me on the channel markers as he called out the directions
I was a mate without stripes learning the marks in a vast blue seascape

Nasturtium

Across the falling landscape of the Presidio are boughs of Nasturtium
Settling on the winding trails I begin to see the August glow of flowers
They radiate a magnificent array of yelloworange that colors a drab hill
Nasturtiums joined by other multi chromatic clusters to paint a Presidio
This mini harbor entrance peninsula welcomes the sea going masses now
How much a colorful array can raise the spirits of those at sea so long
A rising yelloworange hillside welcomes the multitudes that pass it by
Shout a repetition of a thousand hoorays for colors that rise in great joy
The time for a new vision has entered into the Presidio in its abundance
Make your visit and allow your mind to lift the fog and lift your heart

and Dunes of time

The shifting sand dunes on the Oregon coast create a symmetry of beauty
Moving across the Vanilla brown sand are coastal inhabitants of the sea
Fog drifts along the coast and allows the wind to whip in the wet sand
How I observe the clinging coastline as it moves with the wind and tide
Exhaulted sand hills speak to me of the massive changes on the horizon
I must prepare myself on rising tides of life and shifting winds of change
Monumental movements are about to commence going forward..... I see
Afterwards I will redo a landscape of life to accommodate radical
revision No longer does the world wait for us- rather the world truncates
enmasse I arise in the early morning light to ponder whether fog will
hide change Now I will deliberately move toward the sand dunes and let
them decide

Lost Interlopers

We are the renegade interlopers wallowing in this warm desert sand
It may be our telling many intriguing tales for one to fully understand
Comprehend we do not fare so well in this massive torrid waste land
Yet it is the dry desert structures which create it and make it so bland
Dry desert heat will not accommodate raising covers all with our hand
Here we observe sweltering miles of hot desolation desiring to expand
Then transient Saguaro blossoms and Ocotillo orange paint on a stand
A bit later a huge desert dust storm rises and waves across the strand
We are covered with desert dust remnants far beyond our command
At the same time we preserve this Sonora Desert and call it so grand
Should we reject this heat bowl then we must change our souls demand

Succeeding in Our Success

Charge your life with a powerful electric message of seeing your worst faults and shortcomings needing repair
Applaud those working to improve their strengths and letting go of their reoccurring faults and character defect
Observe the several steps ahead needed to get the virtuous changes accomplished in the face of dire adversity
What matters is only what you do and decipher what you think what actions you have taken and real end results
Overcome the bleak darkness by never allowing translucent deep lights of true hope to glimmer, flicker or fade
Success reads in street corners, alleyways, public forums and town squares : Souls freedom drives out bondage

Prancing in the Pavilion

I clearly track all my old haunts where I met and enjoyed a few minutes of mystical music and magical motion
All my fanatical friends were fond of places with frantic music with a follow up in a free for all front row fight
Great gangs of gargantuan gladiators perked up in a background awaiting to do a Jose Greco on someones face
While others remained in the pavilion prancing and dancing to peppermint prangos snatching mangos in tangos
Yes they will reconstruct a face for Mike Mully who lost the fight while girl friend Rita won #1 for Turbo Tango

Covering My Soul

Timing in the Great Uplift

While others bask in the secular pleasures of the current moment and wonder aloud
Pile drive yourself into different new dimensions, new arenas and new self-control
Your life and sanity matter as you continue to assault the powerful sources of Sheol
March to the new music of blended embattlement and charge up bellowing bravery
The new master plan is to overcome the forces of evil on the plains of positive peri
You will claim a victory with great power and persistence living in the Great Uplift

My Spirit is Rising in a Multitude of New Horizons

Change is rapidly causing me to thunder across multitudes of personal agendas and modify an image of myself
I am known as...... yet now I will be renown as a contrasting constellation of continual change and rearrange
Presently my new image is on a collision course with my old self that is wasting away in a yesterday catacomb
Now I will see my spirit rise from a personal metamorphosis in a newform to attack a multitude of new horizon

LACONIC

Briefly

haining is paining	Running may be cunning	Filling has to be willing
evision requires division	Fired equates to tired	Bowling began as rolling
egate will terminate	Winning allows grinning	Paddle makes straddle
osing is now oozing	Charging creates barging	Flowing can be slowing
reaking will be waking	Grinding may be binding	Billows may wag pillows
urling was so Sterling	Good vine yields good wine	Plowed becomes allowed

79

Arriving at the Main Bee Hive

Our lives remain a constant hive of massive structured activity keeping us so busy
What compels us to buzz and appear similar to innocuous intoxicated worker bees
Critical analysis may demonstrate that we just need to be a constant motion to live
Easing into a slow straddle would cause us to decay so we constantly buzz our lives
Someday we will arise in suspended animation and attempt to analyze why we buzz

Coloring the Pink Promise of Positivity

Surrounded by the massive colors of life I observe that pink commands
Perhaps it is a flash that permeates in our mind and then is soon recorded
Maybe it is the hue that blends quickly into a wave pattern of the brain
Yet I know when a child chooses garden flowers to pick a pink is there
There is something royal and passionate about pink that flows so nicely
Honestly I perceive that a certain color shows well in a real fancy vase
What is outstanding hence will be the main centerpiece of all attention
Paint a majestic ordered vase on a primary painters canvas right now
Focus and see how the painter artistically blended a perfect pink bouque
I remain captivated by a subject matter that flows perfectly in my mind

Find the Picture That Transcends Your Existence

In front of my vision field is a beckoning road offering me an invitation
Clearly I envision a plan to travel this byway and discover where it lead
The road ahead has been cleared and my mind focuses on raw renewal
Therefore I will place my backpack in the position and ready my journe
Routes that I choose will determine my satisfaction with all its challeng
Charging forward I prepare for all known possibilities and assess all no
Others have failed but they failed to put significant options on their tabl
My expectation was the road would rumble, twist, shatter and wash out
Come to me road of woe.....I will use wisdom to conquer your adversity

The Gushing Waters of Spring Renewal

The great waters that run through the powerful excited creek gallop now
Rushing in pervasive ways they flow quickly through their surrounding
Massive sheets of water flow with passion to bring about spring renewa
Miles of forest land is quenched in life giving substance to grow anew
Budding promise and upright branches await the grand baptism of life
Gushing waters of renewal allow for the parting of winter as old ice me
Profoundly the temperature rises suddenly budding Spring will arise
Reaching Vernal Equinox we begin the real process of forest remember
Little signs are the telltale welcome of patient rebirth on the forest floor
Arise in the fragrance of new beginning and witness your own renewal

Blend into the Background

Once I observed when issues get sticky most of us become transparent
Key issues arise constantly requiring decisions that we often hide from
I observe that we sometimes cower rather than offend someone today
Wake up! our future is now.. the language of truth needs to be spoken
The twirling ball of freedom requires a delivery that I must stand upon
If I blend into the background the brazen bullies of Backwater prevail
I must rise up in the early morning shadows and speak a learned word
Equity must be champion of the political parlor and enlarged soapbox
If I fail to speak a truth no one wants to hear, I lied to myself twice
Initially I lied because of my failure to speak then when I failed to act
Truth is the painful tack I sit on to remind me of an imperfect world

Churning Yearning for Life

observe friends squirm as they live in a raging and painful place in life unable to assist their broken children and others
choices were made to assist those in a massive maze of melodrama from doing a horrendous free fall despite netting rips
watched people cringe as they witnessed a massed Niagara Falls multiple accident they had no control over as powerless
saw their contorted faces hoping that their loved someone may have survived this catastrophic event in a barrel of death

Hold back the Avalanche

seek to avoid the catapulting avalanche that will occur from the weakened snow masses on Greylock mountain
often My thought becomes focused on an orderly snow melt yet today has become unseasonably warm and wet
the distance I hear a powerful cascading sound that fills my whole being with abject caution and great alarm
n a southern exposure a mass of stalactite ice has broke in seven precarious places sending a rush of ice flying
Warning bells are sounding with a loud clang but the moving rush of winters rage creates a deafening roar now
hose I had warned became the rescue squad of a moment working quick to release the many from suffocation

Hope is Our Exzistence

rials come and enter our total exzistence with a significant blurry flurry to upset all our planned daily routines
ur crisis can set us off like cannons in the night and steal our peace and serenity Searching for answers can

lead us past many victims as we look for several truths Combing our surroundings
we look intensely under the logic trees encompassing us Perhaps there may be a
path leading to a reason for the ensuing chaos entering us Often we fail to see our
part in the maddening hours of our continuing chaos crisis As the situation is
deadening we suffer enmasse in a garden of pain and anguish When the conclusions
are drawn then the crisis unravels into many sordid pieces Climb onto the sympathy
express and allow time and the virtue of hope to rescue us

Vibrant and Living

day I plan a great celebration and become a spectator in this great timed event....thus I go forward into a bubble of joy
odding forward I see the magical workings which will raise this planned event to become a massive splash of wonder
nding those appropriate mini events to send a spark through becomes the critical mechanism to set us on a high pedestal
hen we are in control then we plan our pathway.... it is then I can enjoy the festive fiesta of phantasmagoric proportions

Enlighten the Masses Before You

Can blinding rays distort the images that waver before me then allow me to refocus myself to see reality now
Can the empty promises I receive be accounted for.. then those who own it explain in a five minute moment
Will twin table talkers explain the shortfalls leading to media squalls arising from somber calls from seawalls
Will the map lines to the left lap fine and rap districts and precincts to cap changes that fill gap vines that zap
Should those who take a cake be forced to make and bake and drive a stake through a snake near Rebel lake
Should the cry of those who lie be set aside only to fly in the face of a sty or settled to ply in a sly dry stir fry
Perhaps true vision allows enlightenment only to gnats who have heavy mats that allow compassion to lowly

Filling The Gaps

My life is full of gaps that had meaning and personal choices that fizzle
Gaps are created to find holes to plug and mass changes required for life
I may rebel at change or accept slow painful revision moving forward
Challenge the direction of life or totally change where I am moving
Refining the great kaleidoscope of choice is daunting and demonstrative
Going in a new direction is gap filling and a brave robust battleground
I locate my courage and resolve... tomorrow I start a tedious campaign
My campaign must be radical renewing redefining reassuring and right
No longer can this gap remain empty rather it must fill a remainder hole
Marching in a powerful resolve I am champion of my gap filler forever

Picture Perfect

All created images reside on many canvases that portray a vision of now
Catapulting forward is a picture of artists painting todays lurid mindset
We observe several images that stir our emotions and excite our psyche
Yet we understand that there may emerge a school of mastery in this age
This age of mastery should make a statement that transcends the past
We will arise and encourage these grand masters to seek majestic vision
Seeing prophetic moves we journey forward to provide open windows
A twenty first century beckons a new spatial image representing surviva
At this time we now paint Picture Perfect changes rising into our horizo

Multiple Collages

Multiple collages break forth their penetrating images into my mindset
Monday compels a vision of a Moon Collage that deflects others light
Coalescing on Tuesday is a multitude of warring images sparring life
Wednesday sends masses of messengers forward to herald new changes
Thursday raps a pod collage of thunder and lightnings bare thunderbolt
Collages compete for my many thoughts that encircle current condition
Friday fiercely portrays a collage of freedom, creation and endless love
Moving into Saturday a picture of planting and growing... a day of time
Then on Sunday a blast of Sun penetrates life consumes my multicollag
Charging forward my mind collects and recollects several days collages
I can only allow my thoughts to wander as images of collages reappear

Rebellious Rancor

Pallid is an initial remember message
The faint appearance of new arrivals
For all coming across... a tearing away
A memory of hard times permeates
Can lifes conditions get any worse ?
Yet despite weakness I can transform
Yes once I land and set on terra firma
Then I may arise to be useful again
Then I will arise and locate promises
Then I will arise to see new mornings
Then I will evolve against my half past
Then I will have a funeral for rancor
Then I will then bury my rebellion
All transformation resides in attitude!

Seeing through the Kaleidoscope

Hard times will deliver a blue psyche
Matching our somber moments now
is a point where we feel real blue
here is difficulty explaining the pain
omeone may cover us with a veil
nder the veil a mixture of healing
ealing soap cleanses the sore spirit
nce we pass through a blue mesa
hen an aura of many colors enter

he aura of getting whole is a process
owerful arrays of color splash down
Ve experience our own kaleidoscope
ee multitudes of many horizon hues
healing process has now begun
s we turn a kaleidoscope true power
he masses of change and rearrange
es the mass of coloring a new life
Ve cannot see beyond kaleidoscopes
et the returning colors do it for us

Send for Plato words

see now some real logic of ages
ords passed down on scrolls
ato challenges our mind simply
loquent words design my thought
Thinking is the talking of my soul
ith itself' ...then an action is born
et those words be emblazoned
ow all powered words do speak
am surrounded by my own ideas

Finding My Best Side in the Morning

Often the telltale yawn is upsetting
Not enough oxygen is reaching up
My brain is static and not online
Perhaps there is a need to recharge

Yet I have become too complacent
Step out of my recent memory fog
Align my existence to a super plug
Find the right connection and zoom

Life sometimes needs a real boost
Many have a chosen morning tonic
Prepare your brain for acceptance
The best side of morning is arriving

Send The Best to Beta Droxa II

Preparing for a deep space journey
Ultimate choices are the key people
Team 43B are Adroxx experts now
Quietly they were picked to uncover
Their mission: locate habitable areas
Chose exploration tethers and troxel
We are on a journey to find habitation
Earth planet is in disarray from War

A small segment Adroxx will search
Six known orbs are in Droxa galaxy
Telescopes point Beta Droxa II search
Locating terrestrial perfection critical
Once discovered Interplanetary focus
We are to bring new life to life orbs
Our brightest inhabits the total sky
Today we control multiple galaxies
One day we may master the total sky

Riding out of Ballypoyle

I can imagine Thomas when he left
His departure may have been sad yet
He had nothing to take away only life
Departure was not an option in 1819
County Kilkenny is a destitute place
When hope is downtrodden... look up
He left Ballypoyle to sail to Canada

Arriving in Nova Scotia he beamed
New life to new breaths of possibility
Finding the gift of hope he flourished
Charting new life was a massive gift
Thomas found to marry Miss Mary
They had four sons in the process
Thomas died at thirty-five gladdened

Proceeding ahead into Darkness

Courage is necessary to follow the night
I observe that freaks relish the darkness
Awareness means there is no excuses
Riding into danger must have balance
The ugly side of night can be very lethal
Prepare yourself for some surprise attack
Late at night the loonies lurk in shadows
Question why you are out late and sanity
Allow sanity to prevail and return home
I wait for your bell to ring out as clear
Remember shadows breath endless death

Crater Lake in June

Arriving at the top can be a real stretch
Often we navigate through snow slush
The clear crystal Lake is snow bound
Maybe I was dreaming yet for the drifts
Pristine air is everywhere filtered in snow
My challenge is to visualize open roads
The blue is so clear highlighted by white
June resembles snowcap ice cream cones
There is nothing quite like the experience
I will always treasure this June moment
Circular roads will lead you to a hill crest
Crater Lake remains sitting in a caldera
Formed by an ancient angry volcano
Voracious volcanic lava was spewed over
Wizard Island cinder cone created by lava
A rising mystical body of erupted mass
We can see a stream of creations power
The intensity of the weather gives clouds
On clear days observe its boasted beauty
Locate your crisp new flakes and glow
Crater Lake remains an alpine discovery

Pendulum Swing

Great steel hands gyrate now
A pedal swings quickly arching
The flow of movement in unison
See the tick run filling a silence
My perception has observed it
Movement is a perpetual motion
We are trapped in a timed society
Keep up the pace with a passion
If not be trampled in a stampede

Observing the Eclipse

Movements in space create awe
Populations observe wonderment
How these events will capture us
Experts quote a reason for events
Enamored we only see the magic
Sky magic writes a galactic story
As I observe it we have been awed
Explanations confirm our thinking

Intricacies Develop10

Comfort zones arise by others acts
See between the sands of time
It may be the social chemistry...or
It may be the brains compatibility
It may be the gestures of comfort
Yet intricacies are critical to life
Critical connections develop soon
Other see the wiring flow meshed
Intricacies build on a oneness idea
Growth of ten intricacies fit well
Teams wind close knit and whole
Ten Intricacies eye contact, mirror
messages, hand signal, face form
moves, shoulder flinches, teeth,
Pointing, lurid behavior, coughs
and total body magic movement
Constant and continuous messages
Allow key moves to always mean
Moves are consistent and translate
Translate a clear path to solace hill
Peace driven by parades of teams
Intricacies necessary for code ten

Tenacious Is The Call

Deep is the resound in the forest
A Loud echo must bellow outward
My senses must be perked to hear
Crisp clear ringing must shake me
Otherwise a Clarion Trumpet blast

I prefer the call of the ancient wild
Sound must be natural to penetrate
Appreciate the whole audio range
We are pioneers of the real blare
Tenacious is our ringing attitudes

Yes the call is loud then very clear
Change make practical men shake
Raucous noise blends in our self
We are immune to a constant buzz
Hearing clearly requires real focus

You are called to be great bearers
Find the word to be the messenger

Securing the Bastions

of Freedom

We arrive in the year of total change
As populations grow discontent rises
Governments apply control enmasse
Extra rules and legislation restricts us
You are constantly told what to do
Power from above is laid on the side
We are side saddled in this approach
We are portrayed to look more obtuse
A rise of restriction is a weak banter
Life is no longer freedom but control
The masses are held in nets of nindo
So to manipulate to a certain degree
The chief assembly designs pathways
We are to travel only the secure path
We have become an oligarchy power
Oligarchies rule the mainstream now
Do not resist chains can be real tight
Observe the Bastions of Freedom
Securing real freedom maybe anarchy
Welcome to the breath of humankind

Dubious Documents of Direction

We substantiate who we are on notes
Certified notes deliver our true persona
Our legalistic society requires real proof
You need to prove who you are and what
Now we are redefined in note documents
Ensure that they are stamped authentic
Professionals will audit their real validity
I am who I say I am and how I am now
Pause and review every detail to prove it
Dubious doctor directors will redirect us
My fate and yours is in certified words

Charging the Colors of New Birth

How I envision all the countryside ahead
Multitudes of colors splash across roads
My vision field is in awe over new life
The array of colors contain a new picture
Patiently I observe the panorama of life
How fortunate I am to be at gardens plac
I am planted here able to enjoy the best
Pieces of this birth and rebirth color all
Momentous pieces stand out as images
A remembrance piece masses itself away
Away I visualize specific pieces of beaut
A massive piece I see revises continually
Winds of change sway as a brisk breeze
The wind itself moves the colors of birth
Nothing is hidden in a spray of newness
Our focus : a reminder bush that expand
Perception allows us to see it continuous
Continually forsythia bush as yard yello
Continually brilliant lilacs powder purp
Continually as maple flowers pale green
Continually as Rose of Sharon fades pin
New growth surrounds our vision field
I will remember the places of all colors
Observe the blossoms of birth and rebir
See a message:your short life is a collag

Reflecting Van Gogh's
'Undergrowth with 2 figures'

I visualize myself among all ferns
Intertwined are wild flowers here
Yes here and there flowers paint
Breaks in the ferns allow passage
Walking on a high carpet cools a
Figures walk through lives aboun
I may be a momentary image see
At other times I am a photograph
Then for others a guiding beacon
A walk in the density is pleasant
Be alight for a Van Gogh momen

Music fills my Spirit Now

Melodies fill my soul here
Music always overflowing
Reverberations filled a need
Hearing would render peace
Concentration was possible
Light music a summer night
Rising notes would flow in my mind and clear the debris
The symphony would place priority on everyones serenity
Idle talk was alright after a bottle of white wine and cheese
Find your best blanket and roll it on the grass as a rest spot
Give time to arrange all of lifes simple amenities to settle
Relax, erase your thoughts : Allow music to fill your spirit

Finding the Message of Revelation

I see the luminous image before me in paralyzing light
Surrounded by a city of everlasting truth, light and vision
A mystical image of beyond that captures my imagination
What I envision is a momentary message of transcending
What I envision contains a meaning of massive magnitude
What I envision evokes an expectation of ultimate serenity
What I envision illustrates a triumphant march of victory
What I envision is the powerful image of creation revealed
What I envision translates a symbol evolving to a reality
Then my eyes opened to meditate fully on our triune God
Then my eyes opened to see a radiance of New Jerusalem
Then my eyes opened in a trance to see an imposing throne
Then my eyes were transfixed on what is faithful and true

Raft Running the Colorado

Churning waters drive our rafting
Carefully we are charting a course
The rugged rapids continue to run
There is no easing we are shooting
Shooting rapids deliver us through
Nature has a strong hold on our fate
Often we are powerless and helpless
The river runs its own private course
Our trigger man knows how to shoot
While the river is in charge we dodge
We dodge the rocks and wood debris
A good trigger man gives times thrills
He or she may be a weathered veteran
Their river run charts wild wavy
Ways Ominous boulders are
Everywhere so So we hold onto
Faces and buckles Rapids rise and
Crash our wily raft Adventure our key
Broke as we ride Riding out the bob
And weave river Finding a spray wash
Be refreshing Gliding to trenches
We move sideway Journey is a
Continuous dip and drop We are river
Rats of some renown Colorado has
Given us her approval

Tsunami Barge at Agate

In the haze of fog a long distance raft
Powerful sea currents have delivered
The platform has been weather beaten
Remaining structure stays a wonder
An aura of disbelief entails curiosity
Many travel to see a tsunami visitor
Stuck deep in a sand bar it quietly sits
A crowd of question marks surround
The agate gendarmes request distance
We are unsure what the raft contains
There is a rainbow of intent rising
Immediately prisms of wonder hover
Afterglow of a long journey telltale
A thousand curiosity gazers predict

Perhaps a millennium will pass again
Then we revisit how this happened
Once upon a gargantuan tidal wave
A shift of powerful currents moved
Select parts of one continent shifted
Memorable and known items arrived
My knowledge of Tsunami changed
The Pacific ocean resends items now
Calls of mighty multitudes announce
Recount agates on agate beach agame

Canyon Water Cascading

Beam with the power of thunder roaring
A waterfall blasts everything asunder
Reach for a cascading driving pathway
A stream allows us to envision change
Water remnants flow to a terminus now
We are the adjuncts of the roaring falls
In our time unknown gallons will pass

We will become mainstays of the wild
Preserve parts and pieces to remember
Arching parapets peer ahead to focus
A view of hundreds of miles is possible
Why we were anointed as sole keepers
Chosen to protect the flow of the river
We will never know the elected process
Forever we preserve blue fountainheads

Canyon waters flow off Kaibab Plateau
The mysterious path is often uncharted
Our knowledge links us by the roaring
We are hearers of great primitive stories
The carving of cascading falls writes all
In time words connect natures creation
Drawing on the ancients tales of the past
An unwritten story will pass on rivers
Volumes of the ancients speak in resound

Massive Magnum

There are often flags of warning
Ahead on the road I observe red
I am not threatened I see danger
When I cannot see danger I react
Immediacy of action required now
It is my task to protect the humans
They are delicate so need direction
Thrashing through life's Paranza
My short journey means real focus
Power can be a challenge to mass
My massive prime objective Fear
I cannot allow hollow fear to stop
I live with my imperfection away
My confident psalm erases fear
Total eye contact will overcome
The enemy cannot deal with me
I am an obtuse magnum all about
There is difficulty defining me
The computer windows wobble
Precise definitions fail a defining
Walk in the massive midnight now
I am about being an obtuse angle

Finding My Star -- Quality Called Sanity

Often times I observe shrill sounds
How are we prepared to cope life
Blazing ahead I witness other pain
Compatriots all have real issues
Then I need to find quality sanity
I cannot fix others before myself
What is broke in me needs a mend
Search for the gauze pad of stretch
Soon my healing comes to whole
As a one whole individual I move
Progress is slow initially as I mold
Mold to achieve oneness in being
Readiness to assist others I move
My star quality must be divine one
Divine one compassion to concern
Allow a sculpturing of mold now
Create patterns to heal by molding
Mold others to divine One image

Create peace and wisdom slowly
Allow others to claim their healing
Oneness occurs in the passage one
Draw the lines of star reception so
So a wave of doubt will drown
Quality sanity arises in oneness
Total oneness is an escape from all
Shrill sounds of death will depart
Departure never a complete wave
Waves must continue washing out
We wash wisdom into our soul
Continuing pounding will occur
Courage will enable sanity a place
My star quality sanity must prevail

Tamarindo

Zest was the best when at The Loft
Often I drank only a spare juice drink
Others drank coffee at a coffee house
Yet I had no taste for coffee as a drink

I fell in love with Tamarindo for sure
Of course this was a strange thought
Why be with Tamarindo at The Loft
Well Tamarind is a real acidic Choice

How to taste a Tamarindo to music
Sip to the guitar strings slow strum
Folk music soothes my compassion
Musical words tell a luminous story

I well remember the cultural twang
The songs of yesterday resonate now
Today I am seeing the historic result
The words have become stark reality

Tamarind yourself to a reality culture
Visit tomorrow before it happens

Pale Riders on Pale horses

Flowing in the distance bleak images
I am being surrounded by horsemen
They are coming to align me gasping
Their design mission to take me out
My commission writes avoidance all
My streaming sword called LOGOS
I roar ahead to claim a battle victory
It is a power of LOGOS that protects
Rise on the plains near Megiddo now
Drive pale images to a blade oblivion

Come to Conclusions

Often we fail to make a decision
We founder all over the place
Drifting never allows conclusions
In time others will decide our fate

I must take charge of my life now
If I wait I may capsize and sink
Sinking would take me under tow
Alert my senses and drive forward
Decision making is a requirement

Life directs us to take quick action
We will take leadership or slavery
There are no magic list of options
Be guided to total truth in action

Vision is necessary to achieve one
Oneness will promote the future
Either I plan even if I am unsure
Otherwise legal beagles will do so
Then I am bound by others then

To escape my fate action is bound
Rounding the corners of lifes path
I proceed to a listening bar ahead
My ears need to perk to hear so

So I listen to planners who plan
They profess a patterned package
I am outlined and surrounded all
Now I am a compact conclusion

Rested and Ready

When I was ill I thought recovery
Once I recovered I was inundated
All I thought to accomplish: a blu
I allowed blur to unfocus my goa
Once again I will grapple with all
Become focused is my new engin
I need a plan to wrest my idlenes
Complacency cannot succeed no
Charge forward to the go banners
Change must become rooted now
Locate buttons of accomplishmer
Push the right lever on the left si
Presto can allow for new readine

Collective Radiance

Arising from the early morning light I construct a vision of radiance
Radiance that flows from a certain angle that is captured at day break
My wandering mind wonders how this light flows so intense and vivid
Perhaps it is my early morning perception of this intensity so blinding
Then it may be the mood I am in transpires a certain solid wave length
Yet the reality that bends the light tells me there is a stillness that calls

Stillness permeates my surroundings giving me a specific focus on all
Immediately I must test my brain another day to qualify my day vision
Collective radiance flows in the morning to give us the days intensity

Looking out into the slow rolling horizon is a moonscape of slow glow

Amass a future vision

Daylight will sometimes point to a new vista that we had never considered before in our daily timed routines
There is a zest to discover this new vista and understand the manner in which it fits into our planned spread
Excitedly we find room to uncover the new onion we need to peel and project it into our total days ascension
While the new ideas of creative energy are spinning we find a new joy and vision in our daily timed routines

Accumulated

Over a great lapse of time I have been allowed to accumulate a mass of clinking coins to rend my end spend
Forever I am grateful for the little creep of allowed time I had to create a small bundle of change to re-arrange
Life was a race until my face drooped with raging aging and I needed the multiplied coins to pay my end days
Profoundly I asked to bask a little in the sands of time running fast and find a few pleasing last events to be lent
Now I see what happened to me flying like a busy bee time for flesh disappears I am free in spirit next to a tree

---

Enjoy the Sporadic Points of Transformation
Finding the Rising Members of Mushroom Estates

Gather yourself together and observe the playmakers running the big show ahead
Do they answer all your questions or are they a mass of evading raiders buying time
The pun dents of privilege buy your vote to tote the big moat of influence doters
Our hope is they find gold in the mould and become 24 karat frogs in a marsh bog
Their short lives are lived in the chromium castles built in Mushroom Estates now
We find that they kept everyone in the dark at Mushroom Estates even themselves

I Climb I Envision I Observe I Behold the Entire Atlantis Landscape

Challenging the high hills and small mountain panorama allows me to create a remarkable vision of the entire landscape
There are my new objectives I must climb to receive the critical words of instruction to carry on my mission of alliance
My allies await the new Envision Plan of Revision which I calmly open and read with my excited followers who drone
Observe the landscape of Atlantis we will enter to populate a new continent contently and master the majesty of New Aura

---

Roll My Dream Alive

Witness the carpet of joy
Green brilliance surrounds
I populated it with florals
time has given opportunity
Possibility makes beauty
Thriving among a density
Softly and surely I unroll the bright new dream carpet
Observe how various parts spread their glory power
Observe how the geometry works its precision here
Observe how the order in the wave of beauty abound
I see the pattern of life in power, precision and order.

Charging Forward to meet our Transformation

Out of the paradigm of chaos will come some set elements
These elements will float until they find a valiant structure
Our transformation commences at the base of new pieces
Here it is our focus to begin a formulated transformation
Our lives are borne out of chaos then arrive into structures
Massive structures will provide pathways to new universes
Massive structures will form new wisdom cultures to grow
Our surroundings will transform and we are transformed
Living in the planet of total means requires rigid new orde
Our true transformation will train us to creative IO culture
IO culture will pervade as we conform to be transformed
Locate the pathway and journey onward to Change values

Looking Back on the Road

I see an old road curve behind me
It is the part I cannot relive now
Winding ahead are new passages
Moving onward are new situations
Building upon my past I navigate
Take routes I am pointing ahead
The past cannot provide answers
Brave new treks are now needed
The old road had no gravitation
I see new roads to trek upon now
The potholes of the past permeate
I must be vigilant in my choices
Turn onto Asteroid belt barnacles
Round the rings of stoic Saturn
I amass my journeys a future time
Follow the upward swing of orbit
Heading to Magellenic Clouds
Quickly I go to hyper speed mode
I transition to Light Speed Auras
There is no looking back possible

Scalloped Hedges Awaiting

See honored hedges scalloped now
Enjoy its carved tunnel tracings
Observe yourself in picture frames
March out of your embarrassment
Everyone looks alive in moss
green You are picture made to be
framed Charge to the site of
circumstance You will be the
flower of frame Be confident in
your personhood We are quick
glowing buds now Too soon we
are blowing in winds Glory in the
few seconds of prime Hedges
awaits our true signature Allow
your Rose bloom to shine You will
be remembered in a pose

Sprays of Petite Fleur

Salvia populate the petite planted rows
Then of course golden calendula peep
While little dusty greens line the street
Stem rows of petite fleur color the garde

This is a grand garden of lined brilliance
Carefully planters mixed a strong blend
Blends color the continuous landscape
They paint the drab anew with character

Rows of petite fleur are pleasant scenes
They arrange to be eye catchers of now
In time the scenery will be soon modifie
Enjoy marvels of natures new creation

Profound vistas are created in back drop
Witness how the building accentuates a
The continuous brick builds the flowers
Arrangements will await rearrangement

Our bed of pure painted color gives joy
Petite fleur s constantly color our lives
Prepare for the next colored wonder-lus
Arranged flower beds unwind our stress

Finding the Balance

am in wonder watching the ocean waves pour in and continually clean the face of the crystal Oregon Beaches
idal changes push and pull the objects of the sea in several direction and illustrate the power of natures magnet
ll sea creatures are contained in their limited fish bowl existence to live their short spans on oceans timetable
our forth on the majestic excitement of seas wave to revitalize yourself then find your transformation and grow

Challenge of my Heart

Crossing the dunes
Moving in unison
Quickly see activity
Wind erodes dunes
I reject this change
Dune anchor constant
Yet wind is oblivious
ature does not make allowance for being static now
ature is about churning burning and returning itself
ature is about creation imagination and maturation
ature is about placement displacement replacement
ature is about seeds weeds feeds needs and deeds
ometimes my heart reacts to the challenge : MOVE

lear the Driftwood from Coquille Beach

There is remarkable
There is driftwood
There is Wind whip
There is a lighthouse
There is a new peace
There is Spring open
Then Coquille beach

Arriving at Deer Creek Falls in a Rugged Raft

My son and I traversed the Colorado rapids in a raft
A series of tumultuous waves kept us totally baptized
The rush of the river waters was exceptional in May
Our trip was a milestone as an early raft voyage
Plowing through the raucous river an experience
Roll with a river Rise with the river Ram through all
Our trip was a memorable voyage of new discovery
How we intertwined and entered natures grand realm
Small adjustment:accommodate a rough side of
nature Get ready for tomorrow, swells in a river are
waiting

Transformed by Unity

Allow change to reform and create a magnificent unity   Allow the flag of new deliverance to click
Allow the miracle of rebirth to occur in your soul's core   Allow for a total positive transformation

South Shore Beach

The roar of the sea captures the essence of my heartbeat slowly moving
This sea swashes my heart carefully cleansing anew...a total being of life
Here a process of breathing:the oxygen of accomplishment clears the air
Then a power of nature renews a shoreline to the heart and the beach
After some winter storms I am rejuvenated as my body passed the crisis
Therefore I do recall all the complexity of nature's resurfacing gifts
I am reminded, buffed and awash we all get to meet a in-charge sentinel
Prepare your sojourn along the waters edge renewing your purpose
Observe the gray rocks who act as a barrier resisting the changes coming
Charge through the re-surging pounding surf and embrace your renewal

Horseshoe Bend

Around the curves of life appears a magnificent polished agate wall
Brilliance shines outward and flashes a multitude of fiery tomorrow
Many difficulties prevail as we are not ready to face the painted parranz
A collage of many attitudes bury our passions as realities engulf us
The realities of life often overcome us as we navigate around the curves
Our challenge is to see the wall of life coming toward us as action plans
Act and fine tune our positive projection and mediate the failed promise
Waltz to the tunes that we are familiar with to sit out the blaring balance
Do not be overwhelmed by your agate wall but paddle through the wash
We may not know what is around Horseshoe Bend yet wisdom leads u

Cliffs of Moher

Now winds rattle heavy on the Cliffs of Moher so strong I stay distance
A few brave souls crawl to an edge to observe the perimeters just below
Strong uplifts drive sea spray to inordinate distances which bellows
Never to be overly aggressive I maintain a certain distance from the edg
Those who dare are surprised by the raw power of natures twist and tur
I hear the sound of a conversation echoing on a bluff in the near distanc
Cliff dwellers are hidden using sharp drops as safety nets from predato
I understand the lay of the land and the magnificence of green cliffs
Others use the geography of the Irish Coast as a permanent safe refuge

Havasupai Creek

Here a creek flows in its bluegreen channel
Careful calcite buildup causes reflection
The sky mirrors the magnificent creek
Meandering down from a village above
This crawling creek ribbons concisely
Flowing down it marries to the Colorado
Oh how the excited stream provides life
Oh how the teal trumpets blow on arrival
Oh how the aqua fills the aquifer quickly
We are the keepers of the streams and all
We are the keepers of the blue rising rivers
We must be preserving a blushing beauty
We are the caretakers of this mighty land
And refreshing gift waters at Havasupai
Understand flowing magnificence now
We become the bluegreen people forever
Our land is the jewel so keep it polished!

Victorious in our belief

Constantly we are bombarded with ideas and philosophic premonitions that desire to brainwash our thinking
Through the passage of lifes journey we are often given the means to observe and create our positive pieces
Yet the predominant visionary pinheads continue blasting us with their unconvincing ideas of change and choice
Allow them to speak and then let the beach waves of life wash their massive mudpack out onto the ocean floor

View from Vasey's Paradise

The Colorado flows by Vasey's Paradise
Water gushes from the side Red-wall
Magnificent flows of whitewater rolling
Beauty marks the rivers landing spot
Continuous water spurts out benediction
The land spot is refreshed by the sprays
Vasey first saw this unusual water flow
Amazed by natures path he stayed on
Marking a special spot on ancient maps
Eventually they named it Vasey's Paradise
Our journey allows us to observe it now
We are adventurers that keep all refreshed
We are the river rat keepers of our time
Recording the massive created Basilicas
The great canyon rises to meet our boats
Vaseys Paradise is one place of prayer
We are gifted by times massive creations
Arise and see all the Canyon Cathedrals

A Clear Pathway Forward

Awake I see the early traces of light shine on my window pane similar to a prism arching over me
While today is Saturday there are chores and tasks waiting for arching limbs and finite fingers
Aggregate work piles up and dwarfs our time and talent yet we must persevere revving forward
Change and revision will bury us so we must go into hyper speed to keep up with tomorrows need
Pile drive forward and be transformed into your new configuration we are being retooled for futures
I am being reformed by the secular surrounding access for I now see major reconnections occurring
Our society is retooling itself to meet the tidal wave of promises and piloting new progressive ways
Thunderstruck by an Army of Revision Cadre we are being lead to a new reformation of object ideas
I want to push back the quaking days ahead that contour my thinking but resisting is not an option
Follow the remake of the cities and towns that will now appear as a mirage of futuristic fanaticism
Observe your given numbers, allocations of life giving formats will depend upon your achievements
Be ready to accept your role in the Futuristic wave that is inundating your total transformed psyche
You And I were chosen to revive the recalcitrant culture of conformity and cooperation to be a norm

The Final Word

Our obsession is to get the final word in a conversation with great authority
In an instance the dry words leave our lips with force but fail to penetrate anywher
Communication relies on words that effectively create new pathways of wisdom
Often the power of our words rely on our surrounding listening audiences attentior
Question your words before speaking, well chosen words create attitude and actior
The final word reverberates through the countryside with power and precision
The power of my well sentenced words can change minds and attitudes forever

The Sacred Datura

Natives relish the beauty and bond with the Sacred Datura as it trumpets a pleasant melody to the divining Sonora Deser
Melodious music reminds us that the desert is a place of peace to discover one's inner thoughts and quiet reflections
Proclaim your arrival with the simple flow of music from a Datura since we need a slow cadence to announce our arriva
Rejuvenate and be refreshed your arrival was announced so you may explore a serenity and comfort with Sonoran horns